RELIGIOUS BEHAVIOUR

RELIGIOUS BEHAVIOUR

by

Michael Argyle

Lecturer in Social Psychology in the
University of Oxford

Fellow at the Center for Advanced Study
in the Behavioral Sciences, Stanford, California, 1958–9

THE FREE PRESS
Glencoe, Illinois

First published in the U.S.A., 1959
by The Free Press,
a corporation.

© *Michael Argyle 1958*

261
Ar3r

By the same Author
The Scientific Study of Social Behaviour

37768

May 1959

Printed in Great Britain by
W. & J. Mackay & Co. Ltd
Chatham, Kent

For
Miranda, Nicholas and Rosalind

CONTENTS

TABLES

FIGURES

PREFACE

This book is a study in the social psychology of religion in Britain and America since 1900. I have tried to establish a basis of solid empirical facts by drawing on a variety of statistical sources, such as church records, social surveys and psychometric studies. With this data it is shown how religious behaviour and belief vary with personality factors, age and sex, environmental experiences, social class and other variables. An attempt is then made to test various psychoanalytic and other theories of religion against these findings. It is hoped that the verification of theories against statistical data in this way may prove applicable in other fields.

I am deeply indebted to the following for reading and criticizing chapters:—John Annett, Institute of Experimental Psychology, Oxford; The Rev. Geoffrey Beck, Minister of Summertown Congregational Church, Oxford; David Butler, Fellow of Nuffield College, Oxford; Roy Davis, Lecturer in Psychology, Oxford; B. A. Farrell, Wilde Reader in Mental Philosophy, Oxford; Dr. Max Grünhut, Reader in Criminology, Oxford; Dr. Harry Kay, University Lecturer in Experimental Psychology, Oxford; Dr. John Mogey, University Lecturer in Sociology, Oxford; R. C. Oldfield, Professor of Psychology, Oxford; Dr. A. N. Oppenheim, Lecturer in Psychology, London School of Economics; Dr. Christopher Ounsted, Consultant Child Psychiatrist, Park Hospital, Oxford; Harold Solomon, Institute of Experimental Psychology, Oxford; Dr. R. H. Thouless, Reader in Educational Psychology, Cambridge; Dr. Michel Treisman, Institute of Experimental Psychology, Oxford.

I have also been greatly helped by suggestions and criticisms put forward by my own students, and by the many people who have contributed to the discussion when I have lectured on these subjects. In addition I must thank Janet Burnett-Brown for typing the successive drafts.

The following have very kindly provided me with statistical or other information and data.

Dr. Max K. Adler, Research Department, Odham's Press Ltd.; Norman Bailey, Reader in Biometry, Oxford; Dr. Henry Durant and William Gregory, British Institute of Public Opinion; N. J. W. Hagger, Central Board of Finance of the Church of England; Dr. E. H. Hare, Maudsley Hospital; K. E. Hyde, Lecturer in Education, University of Birmingham; Dr. Benson Y. Landis, Bureau of Research and Survey, National Council of the Churches of Christ, U.S.A.; Dr. G. E. Lenski, Associate Professor of Psychology, University of Michigan; Harold Lydall, Senior Research Officer, Institute of Statistics, Oxford; Dr. Jack L. Michael, Department of Psychology, University of California, Los Angeles; Dr. Erik Routley, Mansfield College, Oxford; Dr. Hannah Steinberg, Lecturer in Psychology and Pharmacology, University College, London; Canon Mervyn Stockwood, vicar of Great St. Mary's Church, Cambridge; Robert Stokes, Church Information Board, Westminster; Dr. G. E. Swanson, Associate Professor of Psychology, University of Michigan; The Rev. Dr. A. R. Vine, General Secretary, The Free Church Federal Council; A. T. Welford, Fellow of St. John's College, Cambridge.

MICHAEL ARGYLE

February 1958
    Institute of Experimental Psychology
       South Parks Road
       Oxford

I

PSYCHOLOGY AND RELIGION

MANY previous workers in this field have combined an interest in the psychology of religion with a desire to support, or more commonly to attack, religion. Readers of their books have been comforted or worried, according to which side the author took. Audiences to whom I have talked about these matters have often been more concerned about the religious implications of the findings than about the findings themselves. This is all rather absurd; psychologists are no more experts on the existence of God than are theologians on the theory of learning, or art critics on the nature of the atom. Psychologists have been diverted from their proper task—that of discovering empirical generalizations or laws governing religious beliefs, behaviour and experiences, together with finding theories or mechanisms to explain these laws. The beliefs of the psychologist cannot affect his findings unless he actually cheats, so that there is no special kind of psychologist known as a 'Christian psychologist'—that would simply be a psychologist who happens to hold certain beliefs. Anyone who is interested in the beliefs of psychologists can turn to page 46, where the percentages of psychologists and other scientists holding various beliefs are given.

There are two quite different sorts of question about religion. The psychologist or social scientist is only concerned with the causes or empirical conditions for religious phenomena. He is not concerned with the other kind of question about whether the beliefs are true, the experiences valid, or the rituals useful; these are problems for the theologian, and with this division of labour the matter might well rest. However, some psychologists like Leuba (1925) have thought that by demonstrating that religious phenomena were naturally caused, they had shown that religious beliefs were groundless, and this is a deduction which many people seem inclined to make. In some parallel cases questions of the causation and the truth of beliefs are more easily separated—as for instance with the belief that negroes have a lower intelligence than white people. Something is known of the causal conditions under which people hold this belief, but that tells us nothing about whether the belief is true or not and research of quite a different kind has produced evidence on this second question. The belief in this case is empirically verifiable, whereas religious beliefs are not verifiable in any straightforward way. Farrell (1955) has suggested that they are more similar to the belief in fairies, and in this case the belief is abandoned in the face of a causal explanation of it, since there are no other grounds. However, a religious person would argue that there *are* other grounds for religious beliefs, in which case they are more like the first kind of belief mentioned, and the discovery of causes is irrelevant to considerations of truth or falsity.

Most of the factual material in this book is concerned with individual differences between people in religious activities. Everyone knows that some people are religious while others are not, and that people are religious in different ways. All that has been done here is to systematize these individual differences. There could be many theological interpretations of the fact of individual differences in religion, but it is difficult to see how reducing them to empirical generalizations can affect the issue.

It is commonly assumed that human behaviour is lawful and that it can be predicted by means of psychological laws and explained in terms of psychological processes. In some fields of behaviour, the laws are actually known and the predictions can actually be made. Alarm is felt when the same procedure is applied to religious phenomena. But did anyone seriously think that religious beliefs and experiences were a series of purely random events, unrelated to any natural causes? It is interesting that many who believe that conversions are effected by God unaided should arrange that potential converts shall be exposed to the utmost social pressure, persuasion and emotional arousal.

As will be shown later, it is already possible to predict with some accuracy whether or not someone will be a regular church-goer from knowledge of certain antecedent conditions, and information about his personality. Suppose that before long it were possible to give a satisfactory psychological explanation for the main religious phenomena. If this were done, both sides could still be satisfied. Religious people can say that these are the conditions under which people come to knowledge of God; non-religious people can say that this is the whole explanation and that they have no need for further hypotheses. Both sides can recognize that their own positions are the product of certain psychological processes, but they can both accept knowledge of these processes since it is reached by scientific procedures.

There is however another way in which psychological findings may influence our attitude toward religion: some of the empirical results may be regarded as discreditable to religion. If for instance it were found that religious beliefs were only held by lunatics or imbeciles, or were a product of sexual frustration, this would certainly be felt to be unfavourable for religion. However as William James has admirably shown, we judge the value of states of mind not on a basis of their organic antecedents, but 'because we take an immediate delight in them . . . or because we believe them to bring us good consequential fruits for life' (1902, p. 7f.).

We conclude that psychological research can tell us nothing about the truth, validity or usefulness of religious phenomena: these are questions which must be settled in other ways. On the other hand, it may be claimed that the results of this kind of research may be relevant to religious practice. Firstly, use could be made of information about the conditions under which people become religious. Those who wish to promote religion can bring these conditions about, others can do the opposite. Secondly there are findings about the influence of religion itself on other dimensions of behaviour: it is shown for example how religious revivals increase the number of mental disorders (while reducing alcoholism), and that many church people are reactionary in politics, and prejudiced in racial matters. It might be thought desirable to avoid some of these correlates of religion. Thirdly, knowledge of the empirical laws governing religious behaviour may help in understanding phenomena which are the cause of undue concern—such as the considerable quantitative and qualitative changes in religious activity with age, and the high proportion of women in some religious groups.

II

MEASUREMENTS AND INDICES

IN order to study the causes and correlates of any kind of human activity it is first necessary to be able to measure or at least to categorize that activity in some way. Some people are more religious than others; what is required is some scale along which people who are more or less active can be distributed. Furthermore, the religious activity and beliefs of people take different forms, so that a number of different scales will probably be needed. It may be felt that being religious is a complex state incapable of measurement. All that is being proposed, however, is the use of indices or criteria by which to classify people as more or less religious in various ways. The 'measurements' involved are not likely to be anything like those of the physical sciences: most psychological measurements are along so-called ordinal scales, on which people are placed in a rank order, though nothing is known about the scale distances between them. In this section, the most important indices of religious activity will be described, and in each case two questions will be discussed—how satisfactory the index is as a criterion of religious activity, and how accurate the measurement is likely to be in terms of actual, as opposed to merely reported behaviour.

Church Membership is a widely used index. As an index it is rather unsatisfactory since it tells us very little about how active a person is or what he believes. Some members may have lapsed in enthusiasm while remaining on the books; others may be keen but never actually become church members. This index is often used for the study of changes in time, since the records are readily available for many years past. However, the criteria for membership tend to change with time: in the U.S.A. for example some churches concealed increases of membership before 1936 in order to evade taxes, while in the early years of

4

the century some Protestant churches did not count children and others did not even count women! (cf. pp. 28–9). Again, care must be taken in making any inter-denominational comparisons, since the criteria vary from church to church. The Catholic Church attaches a very broad meaning to membership and counts all who are baptized in the faith living in the area. The Church of England counts Easter Communicants—probably several times the number of communicants on a normal Sunday. Other Protestant churches include only those over 13 or 14 who have made the effort to be accepted as members and placed on the roll of the church. The usual way of studying membership statistics is via records—based on returns from individual clergymen and published in the year books of individual churches. These are summarized in *Whitaker's Almanack* for Great Britain and in *The Yearbook of American Churches* for the U.S.A. The figures go back to 1900 and beyond. Another way is to ask respondents in a sample social survey if they are church members. Rather larger estimates result from doing this. In 1954 in the U.S.A., 79 per cent of people questioned in a Gallup poll claimed to be church members (Rosten 1955, p. 239) while the membership returns for that year only totalled 60·3 per cent (*Yearbook*, 1955). The latter figure would come to about 70 per cent if allowance is made for the fact that most Protestant children are not counted as members.* This may be because people tend to exaggerate their religious activities, as will be shown happens for church attendance, and because 'membership' is a rather vague term. It may be confused with occasional church-going or with 'affiliation'.

Frequency of church attendance is another valuable index. It has the advantage over membership that its significance is the same for different dates and denominations. On the other hand, it may be argued that the Catholic Church puts on greater pressure for sheer attendance than some other churches. There may be some people who simply observe the outward forms of religion, in order to keep up appearances or not to upset their relations, but who have no real religious beliefs or feelings.

*It can be assumed that 90–95 per cent of American Protestants are over 13 (Rosten, op. cit., p. 219); if children belonged at the same rate as adults, the percentage of the population who are church members would be about 70 per cent instead of 60 per cent.

5

However, these people would not be expected to be active in more private kinds of worship such as saying prayers or reading the Bible. The usual way of studying overt religious activity is by asking people how often they go to church. It is probably better to be specific and ask them if they went last Sunday; the concrete question put like this leaves less room for distortion—it was found in one English survey (Odham, 1947) that people who claimed to go to church 'weekly' actually missed an average of seven Sundays a year. In the case of church attendance it is also possible to count the number of people who go to church, and this has been done by Rowntree and Lavers (1951) in York and High Wycombe, and by Stockwood (1953) in Bristol. Unfortunately we have no comparable interview or questionnaire survey results for those particular towns, but there were four national surveys at about the same time. The results of the counts and surveys are summarized in Table 1.

TABLE 1. Reported and Counted Church Attendance
Great Britain, c. 1950

Social Surveys	C. of E.	R.C.	Non. Con.	Other	Total
Odham (1947) (Great Britain)	4·25	4·5	3·2	2·4	14·4
B.I.P.O. (1948) (Great Britain)	5·6	3·0	5·8	1·1	15·5
B.I.P.O. (1957) (Great Britain)					14·0
					14·6
Direct Counts					
Rowntree (1951) (York)	4·3	4·5	3·9		16·7
Rowntree (High Wycombe)	2·2	2·0	5·7		9·9
Stockwood (1953) (Bristol)	4·9		4·7		
Average	3·8	3·25	4·8		11·9

These figures are very difficult to interpret. The *counts* of attendance are probably too high, since they are sums of morning and evening worship: according to the Odham results 8 per cent of the attendance is comprised of second visits, so that 11·9 per cent should be corrected to about 11 per cent. Secondly the first two counts were conducted in small towns, which have an above-average attendance (pp. 134–6). On the other hand, the counts miss mid-weekly attendance, though the small difference for reported and counted attendance on the part of

6

Catholics, who do more weekly churchgoing than others, goes against this. It seems likely that the surveys obtain a considerably higher rate of reported attendance than actually takes place.

The saying of private prayers, and other forms of private religious behaviour, can be ascertained in answer to questions, but not validated against direct observations of behaviour. As an index of genuinely religious activity, this particular criterion is a good one since non-religious motives are less likely to interfere; as a measurement it is unsatisfactory because of the impossibility of checking and the likelihood of exaggeration. All that is generally asked is the frequency with which prayers are said; the answers could be made clearer by also inquiring the duration of such prayers. As things are, it is difficult to interpret the very high frequencies reported—about 46 per cent of people in this country report the saying of prayers daily, though fewer than 15 per cent go to church weekly.

Attitudes towards religion or towards the church provide another index. By an 'attitude' is meant the extent to which a person is favourable or unfavourable to the organization or set of practices as judged from his verbal expressions. Some writers use 'attitude' to refer primarily to overt behaviour, in which case verbal measures must be validated, or checked against more direct measures. However since attitudes are invariably measured by verbal measures, and since attitudes measured in this way often differ from actual behaviour it is probably best to treat them independently. The objection to attitudes as an index of religious activity is that a person may be very favourable towards religion without either holding the beliefs or engaging in the practices. There is some evidence that this does not often happen. The importance of attitudes is that considerable progress has been made with refined means of measurement—this is one of the most effective kinds of measurement in psychology. Several types of attitude scale are in common use; in each kind a series of questions is built up, from the answers to which a single index can be obtained representing the subject's overall attitude. One of the best known of all attitude scales is that originally devised by Thurstone and Chave (1931) for attitudes

7

toward the church. Another widely used scale is the Vernon-Allport values questionnaire (Allport and Vernon, 1931) which compares the relative strength of interest in religious, aesthetic, social, political, economic and scientific things. Attitude scales as measurements are superior to the use of single questions, since the answers to the latter have been found to be unstable —widely different answers being obtained with minor changes in the form of the question. Furthermore, the process of attitude scaling ensures that there really is a psychological dimension there to be measured; for example if there are high correlations between all the items, as in an intelligence test, it can be assumed that this is a variable of some psychological interest.

Beliefs can be regarded as a special kind of attitude in which the propositions with which the subject is asked to agree or disagree are either single factual verifiable propositions ('Are there tigers in India?') or have a similar grammar, though no doubt a different logic ('Are there angels in Heaven?'). Specific beliefs can only be assessed by asking single questions, and the precise wording of these is important. It is important that surveys should not be compared unless the working of questions is identical. On the other hand overall measures of the extent to which a person accepts orthodox religious beliefs can be obtained by the construction of lists of items on the attitude scale model. Kirkpatrick (1949) and others devised series of items to measure 'religionism' consisting of questions covering a wide range of conventional beliefs and having a high degree of internal validity. The use of 'open-ended' questions can be illuminating: Gorer (1955) for example asked his respondents to describe what they thought the after-life would be like. The answers to open-ended questions need coding or classifying, before any statistical results can be obtained and such questions also take longer to answer. It is more usual to give subjects a series of definite alternatives though sophisticated people often find it difficult to agree with any of these: Leuba (1929) found it impossible to give any results in the part of his survey of eminent scholars dealing with the beliefs of philosophers because they could not understand the questions or agree with any of the answers! The kind of question which goes 'Do you believe in God? *Yes. No. Don't know*' can be improved by specifying different forms or degrees of belief. Previous experience with open-ended questions can help in the development of such alternatives. 'God' means quite different things to different people, so that crude categories are very misleading.

A number of other indices have been used in the investigation to be reported later. *Professional employment* as a clergyman, church worker, theological student, etc. can presumably be accepted as a good index, though the psychology of these people may well be different from that of the keen follower. *Religious experiences*, though relatively uncommon, are of great interest, and are thought by some to be of great importance. This index would certainly exclude many who are religiously active in other ways. Finally there are two sociological indices—*contributions to church funds* and *publications of articles about religion*. The first must of course be corrected for changes in the real value and the level of wages. A suitable index is perhaps the average donation per head as a percentage of the average wage. Publications have been analysed by Hart (1933) and others in studies of changes with time. It may be objected that publications only reflect the opinions of a small minority, though of course publishers and editors have to stay in business, and to some extent give the public what they think it wants. In some analyses periodicals were weighted by the size of their circulations, so that some measure of the number of people actually reading the articles is included in the final index.

We have now considered a variety of indices of religious activity. It is interesting to consider how far these are measures of the same thing, and how far they are independent. Several investigators have validated attitude scales against frequency of church attendance (cf. Thurstone and Chave, 1929), and Welford in an unpublished paper found that the logarithm of the rate of church attendance was linearly related to favourability of attitude to the church. He also carried out a factor analysis of various indices of religious activity, finding that all were correlated together and that church attendance was closest to the general factor, and so may be regarded as the best single index of religious activity.

It is also possible to examine the pattern of scores on different indices for particular individuals or groups. It is shown later for instance that women are particularly active in private as opposed to public worship (pp. 71–6), and that old people have a very strong belief in the after-life (pp. 67–9). Such differences of scores are of great theoretical interest as will be shown in Chapter 12.

III

STATISTICAL ANALYSIS OF DATA

STATISTICAL VERSUS INDIVIDUAL STUDIES

I N this book we are only concerned with statistical investigations of religious behaviour and beliefs, in which the activities of large numbers of people are compared. We are not concerned with case-studies in which a more intensive study is made of single individuals. In this section the scope and limitations of each kind of research will be outlined.

In a statistical inquiry a number of people are assessed or measured along a number of dimensions or traits. Some of these dimensions will be measures of the level of religious belief or activity, others may be measures of personality variables like intelligence, or sociological variables like social class. The relations between the religious dimensions and the others are then explored by various statistical methods which show the extent and form of the empirical relations between them.

The statistical approach as outlined above has been criticized by those who favour individual case-studies. It is felt by clinically orientated psychologists that the use of general traits does not tell us enough about the unique structure of individual personalities. There are different kinds of case-study: there are psychoanalytic studies based on the analyst's notes giving interpretations of the patient's symptoms in terms of unconscious mechanisms: there are the more rigorous case-studies made at the Harvard Psychological Clinic, where extensive use is made of test scores and of information about the individual's career (cf. Smith, Bruner and White, 1956). In each case, elaborate accounts are given of the mechanisms producing a person's beliefs and other characteristics. Smith, Bruner and White (op. cit.) object that mere correlations with personality traits, social class and the rest do not show either the complex mechanisms of causation involved, or the different processes operating for different people.

11

Before criticizing the case-study approach, let us see how far these criticisms can be met. The method we shall adopt in this book is to establish first of all the detailed statistical relationships between religious behaviour and all the variables associated with it, regardless of why these should be as they are. We shall then put forward various theories which give explanations of such statistical relations: it is in these theories that suggestions about the mechanisms responsible for the statistical findings are to be found. Such theories will be tested by their success at explaining a wide range of data: predictions will be made from them and the evidence examined to see how far these are borne out. The point that the mechanisms are different in different people can be met in the following way: it is obvious that people are religious in widely differing ways, and it seems likely that different processes are responsible. It will be suggested that certain theories are particularly applicable to certain types of religious activity. Thus we hope to arrive at a limited number of the more important theories or mechanisms which are responsible for religious activity, together with details of the kinds of people to whom these are primarily applicable.

The positive advantages of statistical inquiries over case-studies may be enumerated briefly. (1) Statistical studies can establish that two variables are empirically related: they can establish certain variables as causes of religious behaviour, others as correlates of it. Case-studies can make illuminating suggestions but do not normally provide conclusive evidence of causality—this requires comparisons of sufficient numbers of instances for the operation of random influences to be ruled out (Argyle, 1957, p. 38f.). (2) The extent and form of the empirical relationship between variables can often be discovered—as is done in the physical sciences. Accordingly predictions can be made of a person's religious beliefs once his score is known on certain other variables. If the beliefs of a person's parents are known, together with the age and sex of the subject, a good prediction can be made; with knowledge of certain personality traits, still greater accuracy is possible. (3) The generality of the findings is established in statistical work, whereas case-studies of necessity refer to single individuals. Each of these points will be discussed in more detail in the later sections of this chapter.

The case-study method suffers from the corresponding draw-

backs of not being able to demonstrate causation, of not showing the extent of empirical relations and not giving evidence of
generality. Furthermore the presence of the complex mechanisms postulated is not verified at all, and a number of alternative
processes could often be invented to account for the individual's
behaviour. How then can one ever know anything about individuals on the basis of statistical knowledge? The answer is that
just as we can predict an individual's religious beliefs with some
accuracy from knowledge of the more important causal variables, similarly we can infer that the mechanisms whose operation has been verified for his particular sub-group will apply
also to him. The more finely such sub-groups are divided the
more accurate such inferences are likely to be.

There is another way of studying individuals, as yet in its
infancy. The operation of causation could be empirically demonstrated for a single individual by studying a sequence of
occasions on which the causal agent was introduced and removed to see if the expected behaviour occurred regularly.*
The presence of an explanatory mechanism for an individual
could also be verified: predictions could be made from the
theory, each prediction being tested in the rigorous way just
suggested. The difference between statistical studies of individuals and groups is simply that in the first case a series of events
for the one person is studied, in the second case the same event
is studied for a number of people (Cattell, 1946).

RESEARCH DESIGNS

Experiments. In a controlled experiment the investigator allo-
cates subjects to different experimental conditions and observes
the effects. Such studies are almost unknown in the field of
religion. The method is unsuitable, not only because it is undesirable to change people's attitudes or beliefs on such fundamental matters, but because the effects would be minimized
under the artificial conditions of experiments. In fact there have
been one or two experimental investigations of the effects of
propaganda and norm-formation on religious attitudes, in
which the usual results have been obtained.

*Alternatively, a correlation could be found between the causal agent and the
religious response.

'*Natural experiments*' involve the study of behaviour before and after some change of circumstances which was externally imposed, though not by the experimenter himself. Examples would be studies of how many men pray under different degrees of exposure to danger in battle, or of the beliefs of people who have been bereaved. Care must be taken in these cases to ensure that the individuals concerned have not been selected in some way, and that the effects of age changes have been ruled out: this is a general difficulty with natural experiments that it is impossible to hold the extraneous variables constant. Perhaps the most important consideration is to make sure that the situations were really externally imposed and not chosen by the people concerned—for in this case personality variables would be involved.

Social surveys are one of the most important sources of statistical material for our purposes. A representative sample of the population in question is interviewed or given questionnaires. If the people are volunteers they will not be representative of the wider population, though group differences within the sample may still be of interest. One of the most interesting surveys in Great Britain (Gorer, 1955) was comprised of people who volunteered to fill in a questionnaire. Similar considerations apply if only a small percentage return their questionnaires. Another source of error in surveys was discussed in the last chapter—the tendency for people to give answers which will please or impress the interviewer. This error is in the direction of exaggerating religious activity. The normal size of sample for national surveys is about 2,000; the degree of accuracy is of course greater the larger the sample, and for the error to be halved the sample must be four times as large.* Various kinds of sampling are used, generally involving *stratification* or division of the population into age, sex and social class subdivisions, with the right proportion of respondents in each division. Social surveys provide direct information about the variation of beliefs with social class, age, sex and any other variables included in the survey.

The use of records is a somewhat similar method to the social

*With a sample size of 2,000 it is 100 : 1 that the error is less than 3 per cent either way.

survey, save that the information has already been collected, and generally refers more directly to actual behaviour rather than to attitudes and beliefs. The records with which we are most concerned are church membership records, whose errors were discussed in the last chapter.

Psychometric studies involve the administration of psychological tests to people of different religious outlooks. This is often done by comparing the test scores of say fifty people who accept orthodox beliefs with the scores of fifty people who emphatically reject such beliefs. It is important in such investigations that the contrasted groups should be equated on other relevant variables, such as age and sex, which are not being studied. In other investigations a large number of people are simply compared on a number of tests and questionnaires: all the measuring instruments can then be correlated together in pairs to discover which are associated together. Such a design does not ensure that any variables are held constant, though it may be possible to do this statistically by calculating *partial correlations* between two variables while a third is held constant.

Statistical field studies of other kinds use similar methods but different variables. For example, correlations may be found between the religious attitudes of a number of subjects and those of their parents. This is a straightforward type of design, but the causal interpretation of all purely statistical studies is difficult, as will be shown later.

STATISTICAL SIGNIFICANCE

The statistical significance of an empirical finding is the probability that it represents a genuine causal relationship and is not a product of chance factors. If it is significant at the 1 per cent level, this means that in a hundred such studies this result would only occur once by chance, i.e. that the odds are 100 : 1 against it being a chance happening. It is important to calculate statistical significance in the social sciences because any series of phenomena under study is not only the product of the variables being investigated, but also of other uncontrolled and unknown factors producing further variation between subjects. Assuming that these other variables operate at random *between* our conditions as well as *within* them, there will clearly be differences due to them. The experimental results must be sufficiently large in relation to this error variation for us to be sure it is not simply due to one of these fluctuations.

It is a matter of convention to accept results significant at the 1 per cent level, though interest is shown in results significant at the 5 per cent level also. For each kind of investigation there are certain *statistical tests* available which enable the level of significance of the results to be calculated. In an experimental study the difference between the average scores of experimental and control groups must be sufficiently large in relation to the variation within each group. The 't' test (Snedecor, 1946, p. 75f.) is generally used when equal measurement units are involved, otherwise various non-parametric methods are available (Smith, 1953).

In psychometric and other correlational studies in which the association between two variables is being found, some kind of correlation coefficient is calculated. When the data meet certain assumptions a 'product-moment' correlation may be used: this varies in magnitude from 0 to 1—from complete independence to complete association. Table 2 shows the size the coefficient must have for significance, for given numbers of subjects. It can be seen that for larger numbers of subjects, much smaller correlations are significant.

TABLE 2. The Significance of Correlations

Number of Subjects	5% *level*	1% *level*
10	·63	·77
25	·40	·51
50	·27	·35
100	·20	·25
500	·09	·12
1,000	·06	·08

(From Fisher and Yates, 1938)

In the following pages the levels of significance will not be given, though all of the results reported will be significant; the reader can refer to this table to check the significance of any particular correlation.

In studies of the social survey type, the results are presented as the percentages of various groups of people who engage in various activities or hold various beliefs. For such results it is necessary to find the significance of the difference between a pair of percentages. Table 3 shows the differences which are significant for different numbers of subjects in each category.

TABLE 3. The Significance of Differences between Percentages

Mean number of subjects in each group*	The Difference of Percentages significant at 1% level		5% level	
1,000	$5\frac{1}{2}$	(3)	4	(2)
500	8	(4)	$5\frac{1}{2}$	(3)
250	12	(6)	9	(4)
100	19	(9)	13	(7)
50	28		19	

(The percentages in brackets apply when the percentages being compared are each < 10 or > 90 per cent. Computed from Zubin 1939).

EXTENT AND FORM OF THE RELATIONSHIP

Some variables are more closely associated with religious activity than others—for example a person's age, sex and personality traits are of greater predictive value than whether he lives in town or country and whether he is fat or thin—though these too are relevant. All of these variables are *significantly* related to the level of a person's religious activities, but the first group are more *strongly* related statistically, and may be presumed to be more powerful causal agents. The two concepts of the significance and the extent of a relationship are of course related: as shown in Table 2, the higher a correlation the more likely it is to be significant. However, suppose that two variables have each been found to be highly significant by the use of large numbers of subjects, then it can be said that one is more highly correlated with the dependent variable than is the other.

The usual way of comparing the influence of different variables is to calculate how much of the *variance* of the dependent variable is accounted for. The variance is an index of the amount of variation in the scores of a number of subjects. If a group of people all go to church about twice a month, the variance would be less than for a group where some went once

*This table has been calculated on the assumption that the groups are equal in size. When there is a great disparity the figures here would give an approximation only.

a day and others never went at all. Variance is calculated as the average of the squares of the deviations of a number of scores from the mean score, or $\dfrac{Sx^2}{N}$, where x is the difference between a score and the average score. When expressed in this way, the variance has the very useful property that the parts of it due to different variables are additive. If we consider the church attendance of men only or women only, the variation in scores is considerably reduced—it has been reduced by that part of the variance which is due to sex differences. In this way it is possible to find out what percentage of the variance is due to each variable under consideration.

When the results of an inquiry are expressed as a correlation, the variance taken up can be computed by squaring the correlation and multiplying by 100:—$r^2 \times 100$ (Snedecor, 1946, p. 185f.). Thus a correlation of ·3 corresponds to 9 per cent of the total variance, and a correlation of ·8 to 64 per cent. When the results are expressed in terms of percentage differences between groups these can be expressed as a correlation, by computing a ϕ coefficient, which expresses the correlation between two dichotomous variables (Guilford, 1950, p. 339f.). By squaring this, an estimate of variance can be found as before. Thus if 43 per cent of men and 78 per cent of women report engaging in private prayer (p. 73), this can be expressed as a ϕ correlation of about ·35 which in turn indicates that about 10 per cent of the variance is due to sex differences. An alternative procedure for estimating the relative weight of different variables influencing percentages is multiple regression. This however can be applied only to the results of a single investigation in which the effects of all the variables are studied; in this book we have taken the results of a number of studies on each variable in order to obtain the most representative findings.

We have assumed so far that variables are linearly related to one another—i.e. that increases in one are accompanied by constant proportionate increases in the other. This is not always the case. Table 17 on p. 68 shows the changes which take place in religious beliefs with age. It is of great value to have such precise information showing not only that two variables are significantly associated, but showing the shape of the empirical function by which they are connected. It would be quite misleading to work out a correlation coefficient in such a case, though the variance accounted for can be calculated in other ways.

THE GENERALITY OF RESULTS

As well as knowing that a finding is *significant* and knowing the *extent* and form of the relationship, we need to know about the *generality* of the results found. If a study is based on second-year psychology students at a particular university, the conclusions may be significant and show a high degree of relationship, but we still want to know whether they would hold for people of other ages and social classes, for different geographical regions, and indeed at different periods in history. Much of this book is concerned with showing how general the various findings are, and how far they vary under different circumstances.

Social surveys and studies based on records aim at reporting accurately the behaviour or beliefs of all the people in the population studied. Statistical findings based on such data should be generally applicable to the population studied at the date of the survey. Wherever possible we have tried to report results *both* from Great Britain and from America, and from different dates since 1900, in order to give an idea of the amount of variation in the results found, and to show what degree of generality they have. Psychometric and other correlational studies on the other hand do not aim at sampling all the people in a population, but at discovering significant relations between variables over a group of subjects who are accessible—often students. There is no suggestion that the attitudes or beliefs of the subjects are representative of any wider population, but it is hoped that the correlations found would also be found for any other group of subjects. As far as possible we have always tried to quote a number of parallel studies carried out on different subjects in order to see how far the correlations found are repeatable. This is not always possible: for example, all the studies of the relation between belief and IQ are of American children or students and were carried out since 1928 (p. 93). The negative correlation found may simply reflect the prevailing cultural conditions under which young intellectuals are expected to be radical (Smith *et al.*, 1956). Generally speaking, we would expect less variation in such statistical relationships than in the actual level of religious activity, and this is what is found.

In a sense, the limitation of our study to Great Britain and the U.S.A. for the period 1900–57, restricts the generality of any conclusions arrived at. Certainly no claim is made that the mechanisms operating here would account for the medieval saints, for primitive religions, or for the Eastern religions, for example. All we shall do is to ensure that the findings have the maximum generality within the period and area in question.

CAUSAL INTERPRETATION

In an experimental study there is no doubt that the experimental variable is the 'cause' of changes in the dependent variables, in the sense that changes in the first are reliably followed by changes in the second. This is not the case with social surveys or with correlational findings. When it is found that religious people have a lower rate of sexual activity than other people (pp. 121–3), there are in general three possible directions of causation. It may be that people who are religious for other reasons have less sexual outlet as a result of the church's teachings; or people who for some reason have a restricted sex-life may become religious through some substitutive mechanism; thirdly there may be some kind of personality which as a result of certain personality dynamics has both a higher level of religious and a lower level of sexual activity.

In this particular case there is no satisfactory means of deciding which is the correct interpretation, but there are certain criteria that can sometimes be applied. (1) If one of the two variables does not change with time (such as sex and physique) or varies in a systematic way (such as age) then clearly this cannot be a dependent variable, but must be the causal variable. Of course it is not age or sex as such which is the causal agent, but some condition intimately associated with them which is responsible; different theories for explaining the results point to different associated variables. (2) If one variable is situated in time before the other, it can be presumed that the first is causal. For example the correlation between the religious beliefs of subjects and their parents would certainly be interpreted as due to parental beliefs or some associated personality trait influencing the beliefs of the child, if the parental beliefs were ascertained before the child had any beliefs. However, if they are measured simultaneously the possibility of reciprocal influence cannot be ruled out. (3) Another method of inferring the probable direction of causation is by seeing which possibility is most in line with other findings and would best fit into a theoretical system. For example, the reduced sexual outlet of religious people can be put down to the influence on both variables of super-ego conflict with the instincts: this is in line with a number of other empirical findings (pp. 156–7). (4) A method which is sometimes employed is inference from the reports of subjects who have introspected as to the reasons for their actions. This may be very misleading, since the mechanisms may be partly unconscious and are often not accurately reflected in the rationalizations that come to consciousness.

The causal problem becomes more complex if we consider two possible causal variables simultaneously. There is no difficulty if the two variables are statistically independent, but if they themselves are correlated, the original analysis is insufficient. Supposing it were found in a survey that religious people tended to be more upper-class and that they also tended to be more conservative in politics. It then emerges that upper-class people are also more conservative—i.e. the two variables are correlated. A further analysis is carried out and the political and religious views of people in each social class are compared; it is now found that there is no tendency for religious people to vote conservative when social class is held constant.* In this case we should say that the original finding that religious people were more conservative was a *spurious* finding. Another example is the correlation found between the number of storks and the number of babies when different localities are compared: the correlation vanishes if country districts or town districts alone are compared, since there are more storks and a higher birth rate in country districts. It is most important to rule out such spurious findings or we shall get statistical relations which are genuine enough but which fail to represent any real causal relation between the two variables concerned. One way of guarding against them is to compare groups of people who are carefully

---

*In fact this association between political and religious attitudes is only *partially* due to this (pp. 81–3).

equated on other relevant variables. The other method is to make subsequent statistical breakdowns, either by making further divisions of the data or by means of partial correlations.

There is another situation rather similar to that of the spurious finding: that is when the second causal variable operates after the first one in time. For example, suppose it were found that although there was a correlation between parents' beliefs and those of their children, this vanished if Sunday School attendance was held constant. The parental beliefs and the Sunday School attendance are the two correlated independent variables here. In this case, we should regard the original finding as still genuine, but say that the analysis provided an interpretation of it, in terms of intermediate causal processes—the parents influence the beliefs of their children by sending them to Sunday School (cf. p. 43).

The difference between the discovery of a spurious relationship and an interpretation lies solely in whether the second causal variable comes before or after the first one in time. This is clear enough in the examples given, but is not always so. It is sometimes possible to decide this by means of panel studies in which the same subjects are repeatedly studied while their attitudes are changing (Lazarsfeld, 1955; Madge, 1953).

IV

RELIGIOUS ACTIVITY IN GREAT BRITAIN AND THE U.S.A. 1900–57

I N order to make sense of some of the later findings in this book it is necessary to know the absolute level of religious activity during our period, and also to know what changes have taken place during it. For example, when we try to infer the changes due to age from the results of cross-sectional surveys (pp. 58–9), it is essential to know if historical changes could have been responsible for the differences between generations. No attempt is made here to write a history of religion in Britain and America; all we are concerned with are absolute changes in the amount of religious activity at different points in time. While this kind of analysis is not normally included in 'historical' accounts, it could make a valuable addition to these.

GREAT BRITAIN

Most of the data available are for particular churches; there are very few summary statistics available as there are in America. Our procedure will be therefore to build up a total picture from the separate data for each church.

Church membership and similar records are available for all the main denominations, though rather different criteria are used by each (pp. 4–5). The relation between membership reckoned in these various ways and actual attendances and claimed membership are shown in Table 9 (p. 37).

It can be seen that the rate of membership reported is fairly closely correlated with the rate of weekly church attendance for the different bodies, which gives some validity to their membership statistics. Assuming that the criteria have not changed since 1900, we can now make these figures the basis of historical comparisons. One difficulty is that there tends to be a delay before a lapsing member is actually removed from the books.

23

An incentive to striking off these members was provided in some Nonconformist churches after the war, when contributions to central funds began to be assessed on the number of members a church had; hence some of the drop in members at this time may really have occurred earlier.

Figure 1 shows trends in the numbers and percentages of members of various churches since 1900. The only body showing an increase is the Roman Catholic Church; this increase is partly due to high immigration, as is shown by the higher percentage of Catholics in the North-West—14 per cent as against 3 per cent in the South-West (Gorer, 1955, p. 239). The Church of England figures for Easter communicants shows a sharp decline since 1930. The Nonconformists increased up to about 1910 and have since diminished; there was an increase in the membership of all churches during the period 1850–1900, and this boom continued slightly longer for the Nonconformists than for the Church of England (Wickham, 1957). If the membership

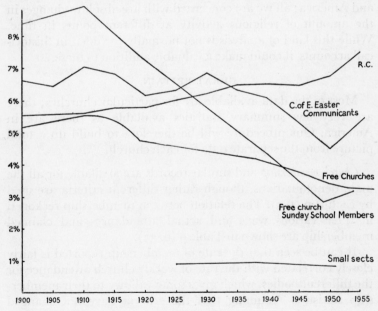

FIGURE 1. Changes in membership of denominations, Great Britain, 1900–55

(From *British Weekly* 1955, and church records)

figures for all churches are added up, there is an overall decline from 23.7 per cent of the population in 1925 to 20.0 per cent in 1948 (Grubb and Bingle, 1952). There are, however, indications of a general revival of religious activity since 1950.

Sunday School members have fallen rather more sharply than adult membership—as Figure 1 shows for the free churches. Since the Sunday School figures fall before the adult membership ones the conclusion is drawn that the first decline caused the second (*British Weekly*, 1955). It does not follow that dull Sunday School teaching was responsible: it is more likely that children were not being brought up to be as religious as their parents before them.

Church attendance is widely reported to have declined considerably since the beginning of the century, but quantitative evidence is more difficult to find. Several investigators have compared the church attendance of respondents with that of their parents, finding that the latter go to church more often. This could be due to increasing religiosity with age, and is not definite evidence of a historical change. Rowntree, however, has conducted counts of church attendance in York in 1901, 1935 and 1948. He included sixty-nine places of worship and averaged the results for three Sundays (Rowntree and Lavers, 1951). Mudie-Smith (1909) found that 39 per cent of people went twice in the survey of London, while Odhams Press found that 8 per cent went twice. These figures have been used to obtain the number of *worshippers* from the number of *attendances* in the Rowntree and Lavers study. The corrected findings are given in Figure 2. They show a sharp drop between 1901 and 1935 for the Church of England and the Nonconformists, with a less sharp decline to 1948. The Roman Catholics show a very slight decline over the period—corresponding to a 30 per cent increase in total attendance, since the population of York increased from 48,000 to 78,000 over these years.

Wickham (1957) reports the figures for the Church of England only for total adult attendances in Sheffield as found in the 1887 Census of attendance in that town, and in a survey made in 1956 through the church-wardens. After correction for 'twicers' as before and for the percentages of adults in the total population at the two dates, it emerges that Church of England

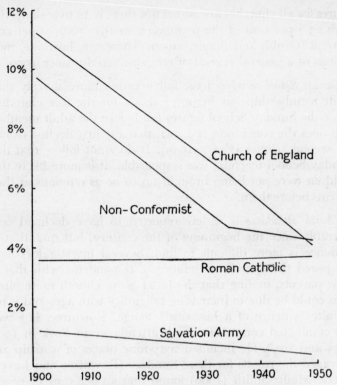

FIGURE 2. Church attendance in York, 1901–48

(From Rowntree & Lavers, 1951, corrected for 39 per cent of 'twicers' in 1901, 8 per cent in 1948)

weekly attendance fell from 11·9 per cent of the adult population in 1887 to 2·5 per cent in 1956, agreeing fairly closely with the corresponding findings at York. Joad (1930) reports a survey of London churches carried out on three different dates, without giving details of the method. The percentage of residents attending the ninety-five services covered was 16·3 per cent in 1886–7, 13 per cent in 1902–3 and 4·9 per cent in 1927. Chesser (1956) compared the church-going habits of his informants as children with those of *their* children at the time of study. These subjects were married women with children, mostly aged between 20 and 50 in 1954; they would have been children in the 1920–40 period: 58 per cent of them reported going regularly to church, 65 per cent regularly to Sunday School. The children

26

of these subjects are reported to go regularly to church in 35 per cent of cases, regularly to Sunday School in 50 per cent. This is further evidence of a general decline in attendance between 1930 and 1954. Finally, Gregory (1937) reports a B.I.P.O. survey in which he found that 7 per cent of people were going more frequently than at some previous period, while 60 per cent were going less frequently. Allowing for the fact that part of this is due to the decrease between the ages 18–30, it still gives clear evidence of the decline in church-going.

Voluntary contributions to church funds are available for the Church of England, and provide an additional index of historical change. This has been computed as a percentage of total Consumers' Expenditure on Goods and Services (Jeffreys and Walters, 1956): there is a fairly close correspondence between the percentage of expenditure given to the church and the percentage of the population who attend Easter Communion: both show a decline between 1910 and 1955, with a rise in 1930. However, the figures for ordinary weekly church attendance are quite unrelated and show a far more rapid decline. No data is available on changed attitudes or beliefs in our period.

*   *   *   *   *

Summary. *The Church of England* has had a slight decline of Easter communicants since 1900 (6½ per cent of the population to 4½ per cent), a much greater decline in weekly attendance (11½–3½ per cent), and a small decline in voluntary contributions (to a third of the proportion of expenditure donated in 1900). *The Nonconformist churches* also had a small decline in membership (4½–3½ per cent) and a larger drop in weekly attendance (9½–3 per cent), while a big fall in Sunday School members occurred (3½–1½ millions). It is reported that 'adherents' (i.e. attending non-members) who were nearly as numerous as members in 1900 have now virtually disappeared (*British Weekly*, 1955). *The Roman Catholic Church* is the only one to show an increase in strength over this period: membership increased (5½–7½ per cent), though attendance fell slightly (3½–2¾ per cent). *Small sects* have shown no marked changes in strength according to the evidence available. There is some evidence of a general revival in British churches since 1950.

Explanation. What is the explanation of this decline in religion in Britain, which is particularly great for church attendance, and for the Church of England? The peak of religious activity in Britain was in about 1880, and it may be suggested that the Victorian way of life with its harsh disciplining of children, and the arousal of guilt feelings over sex, would be expected to produce a lot of religious activity according to two of the theories discussed later (pp. 154–61). This explanation is consistent with many other findings, though no doubt other causes, such as the rise of science, contributed to the decline.

U.S.A.

Evidence is available on several different indices of religious activity for America over all or part of this period, and these will be treated separately, the general conclusions being gathered together at the end.

Church membership rose steadily from 36 per cent of the population in 1900 to 60 per cent in 1955. However, as has been observed earlier, the notion of a 'member' has become gradually more inclusive during the period under review. For example, for the Episcopal Church, in 1916 only 1 per cent of its recorded members were children under 13, as compared with 26 per cent in 1926 (*Census*, 1926, p. 46f.). Similarly, in the early years of the century some churches counted only the head of the family as a member (*Yearbook*, 1956, p. 2). One way to standardize these figures is to calculate the percentage of people aged 13 and over who are church members. This has the additional advantage of putting different denominations on the same footing since the proportion of members under 13 varies from 0 to 40 per cent in different churches (*Census*, 1926, p. 16). This calculation has been carried out for certain years, and the results are shown in Table 4.

TABLE 4. Percentage of the U.S. Population aged 13 and Over who are Church Members 1906–50

1906	1916	1926	1930	1935	1940	1950
55	55	52·7	53·4	52·1	50·7	63·7

(From Hart, 1942, Fry and Jessup, 1933, *Yearbook* 1952, pp. 258–9)

This shows a very different trend from the one with which we started. Instead of a continuous increase, there is now a slight decline to about 1940, after which there is a sharp rise. In other words the American revival dates not from 1900 or before, but from 1940 or shortly after.

Sunday School membership figures show a similar trend. Table 5 gives Sunday School members as a percentage of the total population for different years. This time there is no complication about the age of members, since most of them are children and all children are obviously included.

TABLE 5. Percentage of the U.S. Population who are Sunday School Members 1916–53

1916	1926	1941–2	1950	1953
22·0	19·8	18·0	19·6	22·3

(From *Yearbook* 1955, p. 290)

Further analysis of these records by Pearl (1926) shows that there were large regional variations between 1916 and 1926. Very large increases occurred in the Far West, while on the Atlantic coast there were decreases, not only in percentage of the population but in number of members.

Frequency of attendance does not throw much light on the situation because no data are available for the period before 1939. Gallup polls asking about church attendance have been carried out at intervals since that date, with the results shown in Table 6.

TABLE 6. Percentage of the Adult Population of the U.S. Reporting Weekly Church Attendance 1939–54

1939	1940	1942	1947	1950	1954
41	37	36	45	39	46 (av. of 3)

(From George Gallup, reported by Rosten, 1955, p. 240; by permission of Dr. Gallup and Simon & Schuster Inc.)

It is doubtful whether these fluctuations, apart from a slight increase, are genuine. It is more likely that they are due to unreliability of the Gallup poll, or to sampling at different times in the year.

Donations to the Church provide us with valuable evidence about the years since 1929, for which figures are available. An analysis published in *Information Service* (1954) gives the *per capita* contributions to eighteen representative Protestant churches, based on corrected membership figures for these churches. In order to make valid comparisons for different years it is essential to allow for changes in the value of the dollar and in the average income. Figure 3 shows changes in an index computed by dividing *per capita* donations for each year by *per capita* disposable personal income.* It will be seen that there is a decline between 1932 and 1943, followed by an increase to 1952.

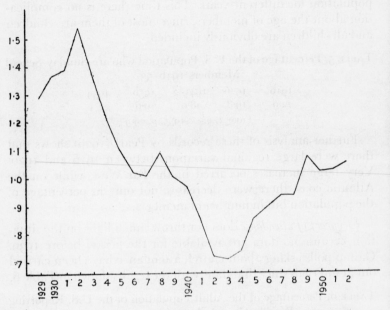

FIGURE 3. Donations to eighteen American Protestant Churches, 1929–52; *per capita* contributions as a proportion of *per capita* income (from Information Service 1954)

Attitudes towards the church have been assessed in repeated surveys on several occasions. Gilliland (1953) gave Thurstone scales to several hundred students at Northwestern University at intervals between 1933 and 1949. There was a continuous increase in favourability of attitude toward religion and the Church; there was a peak for the year 1943—the reverse of the previous findings for membership and donations for the population as a whole. Roper (cited by Herberg, 1955, p. 64) carried out national surveys in 1942, 1947 and 1950 on attitudes toward

*This does not give an actual percentage, since *per capita* income is based on a population including children, while *per capita* donations are not.

religious leaders. The percentage of people saying that these leaders were doing the most good for the country at the present time (as compared with government and business leaders, etc.) increased from 17·5 to 32·6 per cent and 40 per cent for the years mentioned.

Beliefs have also been repeatedly surveyed by one or two investigators. Dudycha (1950) for example gave questionnaires at an American college in 1930 and 1949. The answers showed a slight decline in belief—particularly on the ideas of forgiveness of sin, Salvation by faith, and final judgment. Leuba (1934) carried out surveys of the beliefs of eminent scientists in 1914 and 1933 and found a marked decline in belief between those years. Gallup polls in 1936 and 1944 however show that the percentage of people believing in the after life increased from 64 to 76 per cent during this period (Cantril, 1951, p. 310). Betts (1929) inquired into the beliefs of 700 ministers and theological students. Although the age differences between the two groups was not controlled, it is interesting to note the very considerable differences between the replies of the two generations of ministers. The students had more liberal ideas and tended to disbelieve in much traditional dogma. For instance, 47 per cent of the ministers believed that the Book of Genesis was literally true, compared with 5 per cent of the students; 71 per cent of the ministers and 25 per cent of the students believed in the Virgin Birth; 60 per cent of the ministers and 9 per cent of the students believed in the Devil. Ross (1950) studied the beliefs of Y.M.C.A. members. He found that their belief was a kind of 'passive acceptance' inasmuch as it did not appear to influence conduct, and these subjects did not use the resources of the Church when in difficulties. Ross assumes that this shows a decline from earlier years, but there is no evidence that this is the case.

Several careful observers of the American scene have recently remarked on the growing liberalism of belief, together with signs that there is now a gospel of happiness, adjustment, and acceptance of the American way of life; there is more tolerance, but also more secularism and a withdrawal of affect from religion, while the old ideas of sin and sacrifice are forgotten (Herberg, 1955; Yinger, 1957).

The analysis of periodical articles on religious subjects is a method which has been developed by Hart and by Fry and Jessup, and which was discussed earlier (p. 9). The first kind of analysis they made was of the percentage of articles on religious themes in a sample of popular weekly journals. This fell from just over 2 per cent in 1905–9 to about a third of that amount in 1940, the decline being quite regular apart from a peak in 1925–30 (Hart, 1933, p. 398; 1942, p. 898). In a second analysis, periodicals were weighted by the size of their circulations, so that the final index shows the number of articles about religion in every 1,000 circulated copies. This also shows a decline between 1905–9 and 1931–2 with a peak in 1925–8. A separate study of fourteen 'intellectual' periodicals shows a bigger and more prolonged peak after 1925, and Hart suggests that it may be due to the controversy over Fundamentalism at this time, culminating in the trial of John Scopes for teaching Evolution. Periodicals can also be analysed for the proportion of the articles about religion which are favourable. Table 7 shows the sharp decline in favourability between 1905 and 1934.

TABLE 7. Percentage of Periodical Articles Favourable to the Church and Traditional Christianity—average of Four Studies, 1905–31

1905	1910	1915	1920	1925	1928	1931
77	71	65	58	48	48	40

(from Hart 1933)

Another way of analysing periodicals is to study the number and favourability of articles on particular aspects of religion. Several separate changes took place in the first thirty years of the century. (i) There was a decline of interest in traditional dogmas. For example, articles about the after-life fell from ·057 to ·015 per cent during this period, and of these the percentage of favourable articles fell from 78 to 7 per cent. Similar results obtain for other theological matters such as Atonement, the Divinity of Christ, the Bible, Baptism and the Devil. (ii) Interest in the Church declined. In particular, articles on church work in women's magazines disappeared between 1905 and 1932. The proportion and favourability of articles on the Church, Church Unity, Missions and Sunday School all declined considerably. (iii) There was an increase in the number of articles on the connexion between religion and ethics, politics, social problems and war. This reached a peak of ·14 per cent of all articles during the depression of 1932, compared with ·017 per cent in 1929 and ·043 per cent in 1935. (iv) A similar increase was observed in the number of publications on the relation between religion and science. Science is no longer regarded as an enemy. (v) Finally, there was an increase in articles about Prayer, Spiritual life and Worship—the parts of religion which are based on personal experience.

Similar results were obtained by Crawford (1938) who compared hymns used in 1836 with those used in 1935. Hymns on the subject of fear were replaced by others on love and gratitude; hymns on traditional dogmas fell from 44·6 to 11·7 per cent of the total; hymns on the humanity of Jesus rose from 1·9 to 8·5 per cent.

To summarize these changes, there seems to have been a change between 1900 and 1930 in the direction of a more open-minded religion based on personal experience rather than on dogma, and allowing the questioning and examination of beliefs and their social consequences (Hart, 1933, 1942).

Denominational changes must finally be examined. Members of the Roman Catholic Church increased from 16 per cent of the population in 1926 to 20 per cent in 1953. Lenski, in an unpublished study of the growth of the Catholic population, has found that this growth is due to the high birth rate of Catholics and to Catholic immigration rather than to evangelism. There has been a change in the class composition of Catholics in that they now tend to have a higher proportion of working class members than Protestants, whereas this was not the case before the war (Pope, 1954). This may be due to Catholic immigrants, since recent immigrants, especially from the Mediterranean countries, tend to be low in the class system.

Since the figures given for total membership increase at approximately the same rate as those for Catholics alone, it seems that the Protestant and Catholic churches have grown at about the same rate between 1926 and 1953. However, if the small Protestant sects are taken separately, a very different picture emerges. Many of these sects—the Pentecostal, Holiness, Nazarene churches and others—have increased enormously in proportion to their size during this period (cf. pp. 138–

139). There are large regional differences, some of these sects only occurring in certain areas, but most of the members are in the Southern States and they contain a high proportion of negroes. It has been found that the sects are strongest in industrial areas where population has been increased by people coming in from the country (Holt, 1940).

It has been observed by Pope (1942) and Boisen (1955) that American Protestant churches go through a regular sequence of stages. Each begins as an ecstatic small sect among the economically depressed and socially disorganized. The formal liturgy of the established churches does not satisfy these people, neither do they feel at home there. After a few years the members become more prosperous, the church gets a professional minister of middle class education, and begins to acquire the characteristics of the older churches: emotional and uncontrolled behaviour diminishes and the service becomes more formal and staid. At this point, those members who have not risen economically and socially secede and start another sect—and the cycle is repeated. The Baptists and other Evangelical groups were rather similar in 1850 to the Pentecostalists of today, and there are signs that the present Holy Rollers are becoming assimilated.

Summary. The figures for adult church members, Sunday School members and voluntary contributions all show a slow decline from 1900 to about 1940, followed by a rather more rapid increase since then. Surveys of beliefs and analyses of periodical articles show an increasing liberalism of belief. Protestants and Catholics have maintained about the same proportions, but the small Protestant sects have increased rapidly, and also changed in character, during this period.

Explanation. It may be suggested tentatively that the decline of religion in America down to 1940 was due to slow changes in society and personality away from the authoritarianism of Catholic-type bodies, and from the guilt-feelings of traditional Protestantism. Since the war the churches have become both more secular and more liberal, hence appealing to the prosperous middle class (pp. 133, 176f.). The rise in the small sects is simply a social movement among the underprivileged, and is typical of the beginnings of all religious movements (pp. 147f.).

COMPARISON OF RELIGIOUS ACTIVITY IN GREAT BRITAIN AND THE U.S.A.

There is a great deal of literature about the so-called 'national character' of the Americans, the English and so forth. Most of this literature consists of anecdotal evidence, or reports on small unrepresentative samples of people from the countries concerned. The data on religion afford an opportunity for a more valid comparison between two countries at least in this limited respect. Surveys have been carried out at the same time with exactly the same questions, of representative samples of both populations. The period 1948–52 will be taken since a number of reliable surveys were conducted in each country during these years. Table 8 gives the results of these surveys, including only those items for which exactly comparable data exists, and taking averages where more than one result is available.

TABLE 8. Comparison of Great Britain and the U.S.A. 1948–52

	G.B.	U.S.A.
	(Percentages)	
Church members	21·6[1]	57[2]
Weekly attendance (reported)	14·6[3]	43[4]
Daily prayer (reported)	46[5]	42·5[6]
Believe in God	72[7]	95·5[8]
Believe in After-life	47[9]	72[10]
Could name four gospels	61[11]	35[11]
Claim affiliation	90·5[12]	95[13]

Sources

1. Grubb and Bingle 1952 (for 1951).
2. *Yearbook of American Churches* 1951 (for 1950).
3. Average of three surveys, see Table 1, p. 6.
4. Average of Gallup Polls for 1947, 1950 and 1954 (from Rosten 1955, p. 240 (for 1951)).
5. Average of Gorer, 1955 (for 1951) and B.I.P.O. 1950.
6. Barnett, 1948.
7. Gregory, 1957.
8. Average of Gallup Poll 1948 (Rosten, 1955, p. 247), and Barnett, 1948.
9. Average of Gorer, 1955 and B.I.P.O. survey for 1947.
10. Average of Barnett 1948, Gallup Poll 1948 (Rosten 1955, p. 247) and Gallup Poll 1944 (Cantril 1951, p. 310).
11. Gallup Poll 1950 (Rosten 1955, p. 245).
12. From Table 9.
13. Herberg, 1955.

Some brief comments should be made on the comparability of these figures. Membership returns are made somewhat differently by different churches, so that the national totals are rather misleading in themselves. Some of the British Nonconformist churches pay taxes to central funds in proportion to size of congregation, which has acted as an incentive to pruning lists of members. More of the American Protestant churches include children than is the case in Great Britain, so that the difference shown here is probably too great. Church attendance figures in both countries presumably suffer from exaggeration to about the same extent (cf. pp. 5–7). The findings about beliefs are exactly comparable in that the results of surveys asking identical questions and with the same possible alternative answers have been compared.

It can be seen that the American rate of membership and attendance is over $2\frac{1}{2}$ times the British rate. Beliefs are also more widespread in the U.S.A. though the proportional difference is less owing to the greater absolute size of the percentages (cf. p. 71). On the other hand, the total number of people reporting daily prayer in Great Britain is slightly higher, and fewer Americans could name the four gospels—though the simplest explanation of the last result is that religion is not taught in American schools.

Despite the apparently high level of religious activity in the U.S.A., some sociologists have argued that it is in some sense 'hollow' or 'secular'. Ross (1950), for example, carried out a survey of nearly 2,000 Y.M.C.A. members, and found that 48 per cent went to church once a week, 42·5 per cent prayed every day and 72 per cent believed in God; however, interviews revealed that these beliefs were passive, that life goals were not influenced by religion, that members did not feel their lives had any purpose and they did not make use of the church's resources in times of crisis. Barnett (1948) found that although 95 per cent of an American national sample believed in God, 75 per cent did not regard God as watching them or being in touch in any way, while only 5 per cent prayed for forgiveness. It is unfortunate that no comparative data are available for other countries to show whether or not America is unique in these respects. Common observation however shows that the churches in America have far more purely secular activities than the churches in England; Douglass (1926) commented on this development thirty years ago: he studied 357 Protestant churches and found an incredible variety of purely secular activities in progress. These included domestic science classes, employment offices, dispensaries and clinics, dramatic clubs—in all thirty-three different kinds of non-religious organizations. There have also been considerable changes in the way of secularization of belief, as was shown in the last section.

The relative strength of the different denominations are shown in Table 9. As explained before, the Catholic membership figures are exaggerated, as are affiliation figures for the Church of England (p. 5). A difference which is not shown in the table is that there are more small sects in America and more members of small sects. It is impossible to distinguish these from

TABLE 9. The Strength of the Main Denominations in Great Britain and the U.S.A.

Great Britain 1947–57

	Members[1]	Weekly attendance[2]	Claim affiliation[3]
Church of England	6·5	4·9	53
Roman Catholic	7·3	3·75	10
Non-conformist	3·0	} 4·5	15
Church of Scotland	3·1		7·5
Small Protestant Sects	0·8	} 1·75	4
Jews	0·8		1
	21·6	14·9	90·5

U.S.A. 1949–54

	Members[4]	Weekly attendance[5]	Claim affiliation[6]
Protestant	35·1	24·5	68
Roman Catholics, etc.	21·3	15·5	23
Jews	3·1	0·6	4
	59·5	40·6	95

Sources
1. Grubb and Bingle 1952.
2. From Table 1
3. Average of Odham 1947, B.I.P.O. 1950, 1957.
4. *Yearbook of American Churches* 1955.
5. Herberg 1955, and Rosten 1955, p. 239 (approximation only).
6. Herberg 1955.

the main Protestant groups since there is no clear dividing line between American Protestant churches in this respect.

Summary, etc. The main result is the greater amount of religious activity in the U.S.A. This could either be because the sociological scene encourages religion, or because religious people emigrate there. Most speculation has turned on the former possibility, and Herberg (1955) suggests that many Americans now belong to the third generation and are returning to the churches and other European institutions that their parents avoided in their efforts to become Americanized. A higher rate of church attendance among third as opposed to second generation people would comfirm this hypothesis, but no evidence is available as yet.

The explanation that seems more plausible in the light of the data considered here is that there is a real difference in character between religion in the two countries: in America religion is more liberal and more secularized, and it is attuned to the values of the prosperous middle class (p. 133, 177). In Britain religion has maintained its traditional character, and changes in society and personality have resulted in a decline of interest.

V

ENVIRONMENTAL FACTORS

PARENTAL ATTITUDES

T HERE can be no doubt that the attitudes of parents are among the most important factors in the formation of religious attitudes. In several surveys of students in which subjects were asked what had been the most important influence on their religious beliefs, 'parents', 'home' or 'mother' were the most frequent answers given (e.g. Cavanaugh, 1939). These reports are substantiated by correlations with the actual beliefs of parents. Newcomb and Svehla (1937) gave Thurstone scales to the parents and children of 548 families, the ages of the 'children' ranging from 14–38 (see Table 10).

TABLE 10. Parent-Child Correlations in Religious and Political Attitudes

	Church	Communism
Fathers-sons	·64 (·18)	·54 (·08)
Fathers-daughters	·65 (·21)	·62 (·47)
Mothers-sons	·58 (·24)	·58 (·50)
Mothers-daughters	·69 (·46)	·49 (·24)

(From Newcomb & Svehla, 1937. The partial correlations are given in brackets. By permission of Professor Newcomb)

The average correlation between parents and children on religious attitudes was ·60, on attitudes to communism ·54 and on attitudes to war ·44 (not shown in Table 10). However, Hirschberg and Gilliland (1942) who gave Thurstone scales to 200 undergraduates aged 16–25 found an average parent-child correlation of only ·29 for attitudes towards God. The higher correlations in the first study are probably due to the fact that many of the 'children' were still living at home, while the greater range of subjects and therefore attitudes would raise the

39

correlation coefficient. Chesser (1956) found the religious practices of single women more similar to those of their parents than was the case with married women: this presumably reflects the results of living at home. A smaller-scale study by Shuttleworth (1927) found a correlation of ·4 between the present *practice* of sixty students and combined ratings of the amount of religious training received at home—but no correlation was found between present *interest* or *belief* and training. However, Woodward (1932) did find a correlation of ·39 between the beliefs of 384 adults and ratings of parental religious influence.

Comparing the influence of the two parents, a number of studies show the greater impact of the mother. In the surveys of Catholic students at Notre Dame University, Cavanaugh (1939) found that twelve times as many named their mother as named their father as the greatest influence on their religious beliefs. Newcomb and Svehla (1937) give separate correlations with each parent, and also partial correlations—holding the attitude of the other parent constant. These are shown in Table 10. While there is only a slight difference in the uncorrected correlations, the partial correlations for the mother are considerably higher—this being largely due to the strong mother-daughter relationship.

How does parental influence vary with parent-child relationships? Several early studies of political radicalism found this to be correlated with a good relationship with the parents (Murphy, Murphy and Newcomb, 1937, pp. 941f.). Woodward (1932) and Kitay (1947) found that people who had had a harmonious home life tended to have pro-religious attitudes. It is not clear from these studies whether people who do not get on with their parents form contrary attitudes, or form attitudes at variance with social norms, or develop personality traits associated with the attitudes. Other investigators have studied the beliefs of children who do and do not 'identify' themselves with their parents—i.e. wish to be liked by them, wish to resemble them. In Newcomb's study (1943) of the Bennington Girls' College it was found that the students who identified themselves with their parents retained the parental attitudes and were not affected by college influences. Rommetveit (1955) carried out a rather similar study of the religious beliefs of 14-15-year-old children in Sweden. These children thought that their parents held more religious and their age-mates less religious beliefs than themselves. (Unfortunately there is no check on the actual beliefs of the parents.) Those who thought they held the same views as their parents identified themselves with the parents, in the sense of wishing to resemble them, and were exposed to more religious influence at home. This of course raises the further question of what makes children identify themselves with their parents; the answer to this is not precisely known, but it seems likely that rejection, heavy physical punishment and over-strict discipline do not result in such identification (cf. Child, 1954). Some parents deliberately exert more religious influence on their children than others. Symington (1935) in a careful study of the personality traits of religious students, found that there was a higher correlation between religious liberalism and variables such as intelligence and attendance at Sunday School, for those whose parents had been liberal. Similarly it was found in the *Authoritarian Personality Studies* (Adorno *et al.*, 1950) that authoritarians (who tend to be conservative in religion, cf. pp. 87-91) resembled their parents more than non-authoritarians. It seems as if conservative views on religion are handed down to a greater extent than are more liberal views. Allport, Gillespie and Young (1948) found that two-thirds of the Harvard students in their survey had reacted against their parents' religious views—at about the age of 15. Ilsager (1949) found that quite a number of their subjects later became converted back to their original beliefs. For Newcomb and Svehla's subjects who were living with their parents, agreement was greater for those aged 19 and below than for those over 24; however for those not living with their parents the agreement diminished over this period, as might be expected.

When the parents hold differing religious beliefs, the children are less religious (e.g. Lenski, 1953). In this case the children tend to adopt the faith of the mother if anything (Bell, 1938), as would be predicted from the findings about the greater influence of the mother.

Parental influence seems to vary to some extent between different social groups. Newcomb and Svehla found rather higher correlations for their working class subjects—about ·75 as compared with ·53 for middle class subjects. Correlations were relatively low for Protestants and Catholics taken separately, and high for those with no religious affiliation. The authors suggest that parental influence acts indirectly by bringing church influences to bear upon the children.

All the evidence discussed so far has been concerned with the influence of the parents' religious attitudes: do their methods of child-rearing have any additional effect on the religion of their children? Several studies give an indication of possible empirical relationships here. French (1947) in a study of thirty-nine university teachers and students found that subjects with highly differentiated views on religion (either for or against) had received psychological punishment—emphasizing failure to reach an ideal—rather than physical punishment; however the 'highs' in this study were mostly faculty members also. A related finding is that of Mackinnon (in Murray 1938) who found that the more intropunitive of ninety-three graduate students had been disciplined by means of psychological methods in childhood; it is suggested later in this book that intropunitive persons tend to be more religious, and to be Protestants (pp. 155–60). In the *Authoritarian Personality Studies* (Adorno *et al.*, 1950) it emerged that authoritarians (who tend to be religious conservatives) were reared in an atmosphere of harsh, arbitrary discipline, had shallow emotional relations with their parents and were very dependent on their parents. Finally, Winterbottom (1953) showed that Protestant and Jewish parents rewarded their children for independent achievement at an earlier age than did Catholic parents. Perhaps the most likely hypothesis that emerges from these investigations is that Catholics and other religious conservatives discipline their children more by external physical methods, while Protestants and Jews emphasize success and failure to reach certain standards: this is certainly in line with the suggestion that Protestants internalize the super-ego to a greater extent (pp. 156–9).

EDUCATIONAL INFLUENCES

It is difficult to disentangle the effects of educational from other influences. Many studies in this area consist of before-and-after comparisons, but the changes found could simply be due to age. The only meaningful results of this kind consist of comparisons between the changes resulting from different kinds of education. Another way of tackling the problem is by straightforward comparison of people who have received different educations. However, the differences here are liable to be confused with those due to social class or intelligence.

In the case of Sunday Schools, although there are good correlations between attendance and subsequent religious activity, this could be due solely to parental influence. However, in Woodward's study (1932), later conservatism of belief correlated ·43 with Sunday School attendance and only ·39 with measures of parental religious activity. If Newcomb and Svehla's suggestions are correct (see above) the Sunday School would be one of the main religious institutions to which parents introduce their children. Several British studies cast some doubt on this hypothesis. Cauter and Downham (1954) found no difference at all between parents who did and did not go to church in the proportions sending their children to Sunday School. Gorer (1955) found that the religious practices of parents affected whether they taught the children to pray, but had little effect on whether they sent them to Sunday School. Chesser (1956) discovered that about half the married women in his sample imposed their own churchgoing habits on their children, the rest either sent the children more often than they went themselves (25 per cent) or less often (16 per cent). Hyde (1956) reports a survey of 500 Free Church (i.e. Nonconformist) Sunday Schools: it was found that the younger they joined, the later the pupils stayed; only about 14 per cent of the members eventually joined the church; 'Family churches', in which church and Sunday School are combined and where more parents attend, retained children for longer and more joined the church.

A final point about Sunday Schools is that children who have been members are less likely to experience a 'sudden' conversion with its attendant emotional crisis; they will have a 'gradual' conversion in which they are slowly drawn into religious practices and beliefs (Clark, 1929).

The violent changes of the 12–18 period are generally ascribed to other aspects of ageing and not to educational influences. It seems likely, though there is little published material, that children are receptive to religious ideas at this period and are influenced by schooling of a strongly denominational character—as will be shown to be the case at college age.

TABLE 11. Education and Weekly Church Attendance

College	51 per cent
High School	47 per cent
Grade School	43 per cent

(U.S.A. 1954. Gallup Poll from *Yearbook* 1956; by permission of Dr. Gallup)

As can be seen from Table 11, in America the more schooling people have had, the more religiously active they are. This cannot be simply explained in terms of class differences, or vice versa, since the middle socio-economic groups are slightly more active than those above or below (see pp. 130–2). In England there is some evidence that people who have had secondary education believe less than those with only elementary education, which is surprising in view of the facts that religious instrution is given in schools, and that attendance increases with social class.

There are a number of American investigations comparing students before and after college. The general finding is that attendance becomes less frequent and beliefs more 'liberal'—by which is meant that they believe less for example in Hell and the Virgin Birth, and hold the views associated in this country with Modernism and Liberal theology. However, such changes are normal during the ages 18–25 (pp. 65–67), so that it does not follow that American colleges are causing these changes; in view of the results shown in Table 11 this does not seem very likely. The evidence for changes during college is stronger. A number of surveys, as shown in Table 12, including one by Leuba covering ten colleges, show a sharp drop in religious activity during the first one or two years in college, followed by a revival of interest during the last year or two.

TABLE 12. Changes during College

	Year			
	1	2	3	4
Leuba (1921) Belief in immortality	80	76	60	70
Thurstone and Chave (1929)				
Frequent church attendance	50	37	43	45

So far we have been concerned with 'typical' colleges. Some colleges have a strong leaning towards a particular kind of religion so that the different outcomes can be compared. Cavanaugh (1939) reports on fifteen surveys carried out at the Catholic University of Notre Dame between 1920 and 1935. Frequent taking of communion was particularly stressed: 72 per cent of students became more frequent communicants, and 'frequent communion' was given as 'the most helpful religious experience of their lives'. Surveys of old students show that although the frequency drops considerably on leaving Notre Dame, those who were the most frequent communicants as students remain so afterwards. The first year of college was said to be 'the most profitable spiritually'. Arsenian (1943) analysed the changes in Vernon-Allport value scores among students at a small college at which it seems that a modernistic and social gospel was widely held among the staff. During their stay students came to disagree more with organized religion, to have a stronger 'social' value and to be more liberal and rational in belief. Students who left without finishing the course were found to score highly on the political and economic values but low on the social value.

The influence of a college may be due to the contents of the courses taught. Vernon Jones (1936) found the greatest changes towards liberalism among science students, the least among history students, social scientists being intermediate. Nathan (1932) in a survey of Jewish students in fifty-seven colleges found 60 per cent to be in a state of 'doubt, confusion or conflict' largely as a result of incompatibilities between traditional religious ideas and scientific and other secular knowledge. These results could be due to the religious ideas of the university teachers; Leuba (1921) carried out a survey of eminent scientists and scholars and found considerable differences between those in different fields of knowledge as shown in Table 13.

Leuba also approached a number of philosophers, but they were apparently unable to understand the questions. It will be seen that these results are quite consistent with the findings of Vernon Jones about the effects of different courses, which might simply be due to the beliefs of the teachers. However, the views of the teachers might in turn have been affected by

45

TABLE 13. The Beliefs of Eminent Scientists and Scholars

	Percentage who believe in:	
	God	Immortality
Historians	48	52
Sociologists	46	55
Physicists	44	51
Biologists	31	37
Psychologists	24	20

(From Leuba 1921)

the subject-matter of their field of study, or personality factors associated with religious belief might influence both teachers and taught in choosing certain subjects.

Surveys of students sometimes include questions about who has had most influence on their religious beliefs. In Katz and Allport's study (1931), in a university where there was a strong trend towards liberalism, 72 per cent reported teaching as the main cause of their change of beliefs, 21 per cent the personal influence of teachers in courses. In R. O. Smith's study (1947) of Yale theological students the same number (55 per cent) referred to the teachers as positive and negative influences on their religious growth. It is interesting, and may be of theoretical importance, that in Cavanaugh's surveys (1939) at Notre Dame, the priests were rarely mentioned in answer to any of the questions on influence. Students said that they had started frequent communion as a result of the example of other students, or because of the atmosphere and facilities. In any such homogeneous group, beliefs are likely to be strengthened by the social influences to be discussed in the following section.

MEMBERSHIP OF SOCIAL GROUPS

There is evidence from a variety of sources showing that social influence by friends can affect religious beliefs. For example, 42 per cent of Starbuck's subjects (1899) said that they were converted as result of social pressure or imitation. Surveys of college students show high percentages of students who acknowledge the influence of other students on their religious activities at college (e.g. R. O. Smith, 1947). Burtt and Falkenberg (1941) gave a religious attitude scale to 213 church members; subjects who were told of the majority opinion, or of the views of a group of clergymen, moved significantly towards those opinions on a second administration of the scale. Landis (1949) in a study of the parents of 4,000 college students found that in a third of marriages between people of different religions one partner changed; it is interesting to note that the divorce rate was lower when this happened. Chesser (1956) found that married women resembled their parents in religious attitudes less than did single women: married women have left the influence of the parental group and are influenced by their husbands.

The findings mentioned above show that religious attitudes are susceptible to social influences just like other attitudes and beliefs. The detailed empirical conditions for such attitude changes have been much studied, though rarely with religious attitudes. These conditions will now be reviewed briefly, with reference to those studies which actually bear on religious attitudes. I have discussed the problem more generally elsewhere (1957). In the first place, a person will not be influenced, unless he is a *deviate*, i.e. holds different views or does different things from the other group members. Furthermore, influence is greatest on attitudes which are *relevant* to the group's purposes —so that specifically religious groups will have more influence than other kinds of group on religious beliefs and practices. There are therefore two situations where influence may occur. Firstly, a person may join a religious group for other than religious reasons—he may like some of the members for example. He will then be exposed to strong pressures towards conformity. Secondly he may be influenced by other members of non-religious groups to which he belongs—such as work groups or educational groups; this is a more common situation, but here the pressures will be weaker since religion is not relevant to the group purposes. The mechanism whereby deviates conform is probably via the process of rejection of deviates; people discover that deviation leads to rejection and conform in order to be accepted. The reason why the other members want deviates to conform is less obvious. In some groups the group goals will not be attained unless the members act in parallel—as in the case of work groups, whose rates may be cut if anyone works too hard. Why should conformity of beliefs be required? Festinger (1954) has suggested that people need social support for their beliefs, and create such support by enforcing conformity. The study by Festinger and others (1956) of an end-of-the-world cult, shows how clear disconfirmation of a belief in physical terms (i.e. the world did not come to an end) can lead to increased proselytization—as predicted by the social support hypothesis.

Social influence is greater when the group is a *reference group* for a person, i.e. when he is keen to be accepted as a member of the group. Newcomb (1943) found more political conformity in a girls' college for the girls who were more concerned with acceptance at college than with acceptance at home; Rommetveit (1955), as described earlier, found more conformity in schoolchildren on religious matters when they were less keen to resemble their parents. It is interesting that these children thought that their peers held less orthodox beliefs than themselves whereas on average they must have held the same beliefs. R. O. Smith (1947) found that 48 per cent of the theological students surveyed regarded their fellow students as a negative influence in religious matters, while only 5 per cent regarded them as a positive influence. These results would be accounted for by assuming that the subjects in each case were becoming more orthodox as a result of adult influences. Then the students might tend to conceal their growing orthodoxy from one another and thus exert a negative influence. In the Notre Dame surveys (Cavanaugh, 1939) students were mentioned most often as the cause of more frequent taking of communion—no mention is made of the teaching staff, as in the studies of Protestant students.

Some people are more susceptible to social influences than others: probably authoritarians and neurotics (apart from obsessionals) are more easily influenced. M. B. Smith and others (1956) distinguish those people whose attitudes are primarily an adjustment to group standards from those whose attitudes are based more on internal personality dynamics. The former change their beliefs rapidly as they join new groups, whereas the others do not.

Groups can exert more influence over activities that are publicly observable by the group members, as several experiments show. Sometimes views are expressed in public which are different from those held in private: Schanck (1932) studied

48

a keen Methodist community where people disapproved of tobacco, alcohol and cards although many of the members indulged privately in these same things. It is noteworthy that religious *beliefs* are strictly unobservable since it is literally impossible to discover if a person really believes something or not.

Although people may first acquire attitudes through overt conformity to group standards, after a time *internationalization* takes place; then private as well as public attitudes are affected. The internationalization of parental standards is associated with the formation of a super-ego; the internalization of group standards probably works in a similar way.

Social influence is greatest on beliefs which are vague and unstructured, and on matters about which the subject is ignorant. The contents of religious beliefs are extremely vague—as is shown by the diversity of interpretations given to the idea of the after-life (Gorer, 1955). Matters of religious practice—ritual, organization, etc.—are much more definite, and it would be expected that agreement over them would be more difficult.

WAR EXPERIENCE

The most interesting problem here concerns the impact of stress in battle on religious behaviour. Valuable evidence is provided by Stouffer and his colleagues (1949) who report on the surveys carried out in the American Army during the last war. About 75 per cent of men were helped 'a lot' by prayer 'when the going was tough', which was higher than the percentage mentioning other responses such as thinking of not letting the other man down, feeling hatred for the enemy, or thinking about what they were fighting for. The men who were most exposed to stress in battle were helped by prayer in a higher percentage of cases: infantrymen mentioned this more than men in other branches, as did those who had seen friends killed or who had been shelled or bombed by their own side. There was some evidence that men whose resources for dealing with stress were less adequate were helped by prayer more: replacements, who would have less group support, said more frequently that prayer helped them. Similarly, men who were most frightened in battle said they were helped by prayer in 72 per cent of cases, as compared with 42 per cent for those least frightened; this was also true for the men with least confidence in battle, those who were least willing to take part in more fighting, and those most concerned about becoming a casualty. As the authors point out, it is possible though unlikely that the use of prayer made the men more afraid, instead of the reverse. It seems most likely that both objective and subjective stress are related to prayer as a response. Men in the ranks prayed rather more than N.C.O.s or officers, but educational differences did not affect the use of prayer. It is interesting that other mental adjustments to stress, such as the thought of not letting the other man down, followed a quite different statistical pattern: this was less often mentioned by men who had been under stress and who showed neurotic symptoms.

Since prayer was found helpful in battle by so many soldiers, it would be expected that ex-servicemen would be more religious than before. Table 14A shows the results of three surveys in which soldiers were asked if their war experiences had made them more or less religious.

TABLE 14. The Effect of War Experience on Religion

A. *"Being Religious"*

	More religious	No effect	Less religious
Princeton Students (Crespi & Shapleigh, reported by Allport et al. 1948)	25·1	53·3	18·6
Harvard Students (Allport et al. 1948)	26·3	54·5	19·2
U.S. Army Survey (Stouffer et al. 1949, p. 187)			
(1) Men with combat experience	29	41	30
(2) Men without combat experience	23	42	35

B. *Interest in Problems of Religion*

	More interested	No effect	Less interested
Harvard Students (loc. cit.)	58·4	36·7	4·9

C. *Belief in God*

	Increased faith	No effect	Decreased faith
U.S. Army Survey (loc. cit.)			
(1) Men with combat experience	79	2	19
(2) Men without combat experience	54	29	17

One striking result is that similar experiences can have opposite effects on different men. Allport, Gillespie and Young (1948) report some of the reasons given by their subjects for changes in religious beliefs. Those who had become less religious said that the horrors of war, together with seeing churchgoers killed, had made them sceptical; those who had become more religious referred to the help they had had from prayer in battle. About equal numbers in these surveys claim to have become more and less 'religious', but comparisons of ex-service students with others show that the former have a less favourable attitude towards the church (Telford, 1950), attend church less frequently and hold less orthodox religious views (Allport op. cit.). When we look at other criteria, different results appear. According to the Army survey, there is an increased belief in God, and the Harvard students said they were more interested in problems of religion than before. Allport concludes that although war experience weakens traditional church religion, it increases the concern with basic religious ideas. The previous findings on prayer receive some confirmation in that men who had been in action reported that they were more religious and had an increased faith more often than those who had not been in action (Table 14C).

Finally, we can inquire how far national interest in religion was affected in wartime. The best available data are for the U.S.A. during the last war. As shown previously, church attendance was lower during this period than either before or after, as were donations to church funds. The revival in American religion appears to date from the war, whereas there had been a continual decline since the turn of the century (pp. 28–34). It is possible however that this is part of a larger trend due to quite different sociological causes. In Great Britain there has been a gradual decline since 1920 which has only recently been reversed (pp. 23–34). Data for the 1914–18 war are not very accurate, but there is no evidence in either country of any marked effect.

EVANGELISTIC MEETINGS

Attitudes and beliefs can be influenced by verbal communications; these can be delivered face-to-face at public meetings or via the mass media of radio, television and print. Although the mass media reach a wider audience, the effect on that audience is less than at public meetings—the traditional vehicle for religious evangelism. Wilke (1934) measured the attitudes of 341 students towards the existence of God before and after they had heard a ten-minute speech. Those students who had heard the speaker in person changed their attitudes considerably more than others who heard the same speech through a loudspeaker or read it in print. Later studies investigating other kinds of attitude show a slight superiority of lectures heard direct over those heard through a loudspeaker, and find that oral presentation is more effective than written. The general literature on propaganda is reviewed by Murphy, Murphy and Newcomb (1937) and Hovland (1954); in this section brief reference will be made to the general results, as well as to findings about changes of religious attitudes in particular. As Hovland suggests (loc. cit.), the superiority of face-to-face presentation could be due to the added visual element, to a greater flexibility through observation of the audience's response, to the better attraction of attention, or to the increased pressure due to personal contact.

Experimental studies of emotional versus rational propaganda have failed to show any consistent results. In real-life situations emotional appeals seem to be more effective, as for example in Hartmann's study (1936) of political propaganda. Sargant (1957) puts forward the interesting hypothesis that the most effective techniques first create states of emotional exhaustion in the hearers, and that people are extremely suggestible when in this condition. He lists the different methods of producing such exhaustion in different religious groups—the prolonged rhythmic dancing and drumming of Voodoo, the handling of poisonous snakes in Tennessee snake cults, and the deliberate concentration of excited evangelists on intended converts in small Protestant sects. Sargant maintains that people are suggestible to anything when emotionally fatigued, and reports that certain young men attend snake-cult meetings in order to seduce girls who have just been saved—they are just as easily seduced as saved at this juncture.

Some support for Sargant's hypothesis may be obtained by a comparison of the efficacy of different methods of evangelism.

52

In the early days of revivalism in America and in campaigns like John Wesley's in England, wild emotional scenes were frequently reported. The evangelist would preach in a way calculated to produce great anxiety—'I preach hell because it arouses their fears, arrests their consciences and causes them to reform their lives and habits. . . . Hell has been running for six thousand years. It is filling up every day. Where is it? About eighteen miles from here. Which way is it? Straight down—not over eighteen miles, down in the bowels of the earth'. (From Pratt, 1924, p. 178.) The emotions were further stirred by the singing of very moving hymns. The result was often devastating, hundreds of those present would speak with tongues or bark, display violent jerking, and twitching, while many collapsed senseless on the ground (Davenport, 1906). No figures are available, but the reports of these meetings indicate that a high proportion of those present were affected in the ways described and were converted, temporarily at least.

This kind of evangelism is rare nowadays outside small sects and American negro churches, and a more sedate form of evangelism has taken its place. The most spectacular examples of this in England are the three campaigns of Billy Graham in 1954–5, about which a certain amount of statistical and descriptive evidence is available.* The most startling aspect of these campaigns is the number of people affected: about $5\frac{1}{2}$ million attended these three campaigns, though some went more than once—it was estimated that half the audience were new at each meeting, which would cut the above figure to half. About 120,000 came forward and made 'decisions for Christ' of whom 75 per cent were making their first public decision and 61 per cent were not already church members—though according to Herron's survey (1955) only 48·6 per cent were genuine non-churchgoers. Thus about one person in fifty came forward, one in a hundred being a genuine convert; this percentage is probably much lower than for the earlier evangelists, supporting Sargant's hypothesis—although the total numbers involved were large. Two-thirds of those making decisions were women, and 60 per cent were under 19. Only 16 per cent regarded themselves as belonging to small sects or 'evangelical' churches;

*I am indebted to Dr. Erik Routley of Mansfield College, Oxford, for giving me access to his collection of newspaper cuttings on this subject.

47 per cent were Nonconformist, 37 per cent Church of England.

What is the technique responsible for these prodigious numbers of conversions? Several factors may be suggested, and given some support from the quantitative and descriptive material available. (*a*) There was an elaborate public relations campaign before the meetings, by posters and other publications, by a film, and via the churches. The prestige built up for Billy Graham is no doubt a factor in the higher percentage of converts at his meetings as opposed to those by other members of his team (Table 15). About half the seats were booked by parties, mostly from churches, and many people went with the intention of making a public decision. (*b*) Considerable use was made of music—highly emotional gospel hymns sung by the many thousands present, assisted by a choir of 1,500 and by various American singers. This partly explains why a much lower percentage of people came forward at the relay meetings (Table 15). (*c*) Graham's forty-minute addresses avoided hell-fire and were less emotional than those of many evangelists; however he was much concerned with sin and worldly pleasures, made use of the fear of death ('in ten years a quarter of you will be dead'), and indulged in repetition and other oratorical devices; he gave a strong impression of sincerity and conviction. (*d*) The address led up to the appeal to come forward to make a decision; applause was forbidden and Alistair Cooke (1955), writing in the *Manchester Guardian*, suggests that coming forward was the only way of gaining emotional release. The sight of up to 3,000 people going forward would have a powerful suggestive effect: this may be the reason why the larger meetings at Wembley were the most successful (Table 15). There were no wild scenes as in earlier revivals, but many of those going forward were clearly emotionally moved. (*e*) All those making decisions were met by counsellors, and cards giving their details were sent to the appropriate local clergyman, who was supposed to integrate them into his church.

The next question to be raised concerns the permanence of evangelical conversions. Two careful follow-up studies have been carried out of Graham's campaigns, and these will be discussed first. Highet (1957) carried out censuses of church attendance in Glasgow before and after the campaign. Weekly

TABLE 15. Percentages of Audiences Responding at Billy Graham's Meetings

	Average size of meeting	Number of meetings	Percentage making decisions
Graham's Harringay meetings 1954. First four weeks	11,600	33	2·30
Relay Services during 1954 campaign	930	430	0·44
Meetings addressed by members of Graham's team 1954	410	425	1·15
Graham's Glasgow meetings 1955	16,000	16	2·39
Graham's Wembley meetings 1955	56,000	8	5·30

(Computed from various figures given in Colquhoun, 1955, and from figures released by the Campaign organization.)

attendance rose by 10,575 from 7·6 to 9·2 per cent of the adult population just after the campaign, and 4,197 new members came on to the church records during the next few months. However, a census of attendance carried out a year after the campaign showed that only 54 per cent of the new attenders were still going to church. Herron (1955) sent a questionnaire to 1,500 vicars listed by the Graham organization, after the Harringay campaign. Of these, 520 replied giving details of 3,222 individuals for whom cards had been received. It was found that 64 per cent of the people who had previously not been church-goers were still attending about eight months after the campaign. This is consistent with the first in suggesting that about half the real converts are active a year later.

Starbuck (1899) reported that 87 per cent of a group of ninety-two revival converts had lapsed within six months, compared with 40 per cent of a group of 'gradual' converts. Wilson (1955) reports that at Elim Foursquare Gospel meetings in England after the war, about one in six of those converted actually become members of the church. This is consistent with

55

Starbuck's finding that about one in eight is left after six months. We may suggest that just as a higher percentage of people respond at these highly emotional revival meetings, so these conversions are more short-lived.

It is very hard to say what personality factors produce successful evangelists. While there are plenty of cases on record of revivalist preachers and other religious leaders who were deeply disturbed, even psychotic (pp. 109–11), there are others who were not. Two things at least are required, a passionate, perhaps fanatical, religious conviction, and a flair for public speaking. While the violent religious experiences of the psychotic may give him conviction and perhaps prestige, his psychosis would prevent him being sufficiently sensitive to an audience to make an effective speaker. Experimental studies have shown the importance of the prestige of a speaker, as did the Billy Graham results.

It is often supposed that simple one-sided messages are the most effective. Cantril (1941) stresses the over-simplifications used in successful movements such as the Kingdom of Father Divine and the Townsend plan. It may be the case that such simple solutions are eagerly accepted by many people who find the true situation too puzzling. However there is some evidence from research on international attitudes that presentation of both sides of the case is more effective with those who are initially opposed to the case being presented, and also with the more intelligent. In the old-fashioned revival the speaker convinced his hearers that they were certain to go to hell—ending with a simple prescription for avoiding this.

Some members of the audience are affected more than others: what are the personality variables associated with susceptibility? Evidence drawn from actual studies of conversion shows that people converted at public meetings are more easily hypnotized, display more motor automatisms and can therefore be classified to some extent as hysterics (pp. 86–87), Cantril (1940) found that the people most affected by Orson Welles's 'Invasion from Mars' broadcast were also more religious than those not affected, and were more suggestible and less intelligent. Experimental work on propaganda suggests that people most easily influenced are low in self-esteem—they have an undue fear of social disapproval and are correspondingly easily influenced. Cantril's conclusion that they are also less intelligent has also been confirmed by a number of studies.

Summary for Chapter 5. (*a*) There is a correlation of about ·3–·5 between measures of the religious activities or attitudes of parents and their children, when the latter are of student age. The correlation is higher when the children like their parents, when the children live at home, with the attitude of the mother, and when the parents are religious conservatives. There is some evidence that Catholics receive more physical discipline, while Protestants and Jews are exhorted to reach certain standards.

(*b*) Sunday School attendance is not related to parental religious practices, and influences the beliefs of children. Secondary and college education has various effects varying with the establishment and with the subjects studied; this is due to the influence of the teachers and the other students. American students show a temporary decline in religious activity during the middle years of college. There is little overall effect of education as such.

(*c*) Religious attitudes and beliefs are influenced by group pressures as in the case of other attitudes. This happens particularly when a person is keen to be accepted by the group, for publicly observable behaviour, and in the case of authoritarians.

(*d*) A majority of soldiers are helped by prayer, particularly when under great stress. Ex-servicemen are on the whole more interested in religious problems and have a greater belief in God, but go to church less.

(*e*) The more emotional evangelistic meetings produce many converts, but only about 15 per cent are permanent. In meetings of the Billy Graham type, 2–5 per cent of those present make 'decisions', and 50 per cent of these are still active a year later. Factors in producing such conversions are the skill and prestige of the speaker, the size of the meeting, and the preparatory and follow-up organization.

Direction of Causation. It can be assumed in most of these studies that the environmental factor is the causal agent.

Explanation. All these findings can be regarded as instances of social learning, mediated by the usual processes of persuasion, imitation and norm-formation (pp. 143–5).

VI

RELIGION AND AGE

THE variation of religious activity and beliefs with age is one of the most important of the problems to be considered in this book, and it throws considerable light on psychological processes. Several of the theories to be discussed later are primarily concerned with the explanation of the changes which occur during adolescence. The age variable is on the face of it a simple one—compared with some of the more complex ones to be dealt with in later chapters. However for some purposes *mental age* is a more illuminating variable than chronological age: a child's mental age is the average chronological age of children showing the same degree of intelligence, as measured by mental tests. It would be illuminating to develop a similar index of senility—to allow for the fact that some people 'age' faster than others—but so far this has not been done.

When age differences in attitudes are found in a cross-sectional survey, it is sometimes possible to account for them by historical factors. For example, there is a steady increase with age in voting Conservative in Great Britain: if we assume that many people form their political attitudes during their youth and never change them, then it may be noted that the older people nowadays are less likely to have acquired Labour attitudes, since the Labour Party had little influence during their youth. In the present section, therefore, it is important to keep an eye on the historical changes reviewed in the last chapter. Apart from this alternative explanation of age changes, the direction of causation is clear: age, or rather factors associated with age, are responsible for the changes in religious activity. It is, however, much more difficult to decide which of the many factors associated with age is responsible; this will be discussed in the theoretical section later.

There are two main kinds of statistical research on ageing.

58

In one, people of different ages are compared—as in social surveys and other cross-sectional comparisons of particular groups. In the other, subjects are asked about their past and present religious activities. These longitudinal studies can supply important supplementary information, since the survey design may conceal opposite trends among different sub-groups, which do not affect the total score. It will be seen that this happens between the ages 12–18.

CHILDHOOD (3–10)

During this period there is considerable religious activity. This is partly from environmental causes—many children have parents who are religious, while many who do not are sent to Sunday School (pp. 39f, 43). Harms (1944) analysed several thousand drawings made by children who were asked to draw their idea of God. No statistical analysis is presented, but it is reported that in the 3–6 period the drawings were fairly uniform: they all showed a kind of fairy-tale person in flowing robes. Several investigators have reported that religion is like a fairy-tale to children of this age; they like the Bible stories and accept them in this spirit. However, a good deal of awe is attached to the idea of God, and he may be thought of as like the child's own father. In the early years 3–6, children may have all manner of grotesque fantasies, usually of an egocentric nature; they will say their prayers, usually asking for the gratification of childish desires (Kupky, 1928). During the period 6–10 children come to learn and to accept without questioning the standard religious ideas of their social group. Bose (1929) found an increasingly accurate knowledge of the meaning of religious concepts over the period 8–15, and that this was greater for the more intelligent. Harms (op. cit.) found a high degree of acceptance of conventional ideas in the 6–10 group; these children also had more realistic beliefs as compared with the 3–6 children with their fairy-tale conceptions.

ADOLESCENCE (10–18)

The period 10–18, which we will label 'adolescence', is of very great interest. It is the age of religious awakening, during

which time people either become converted or decide to abandon the faith of their childhood, if they had one.

The best known kind of investigation is that in which religious people aged 18 or over are asked for details of how they
became religious. There have been many such investigations,
beginning with Starbuck's (1899); thirty-two studies are reviewed by Mckeefery (1949). It is found that 30 per cent of
religious people report a more or less sudden conversion experience, while the others became gradually more religious as a
result of social influences. If we count only those reporting a
'definite crisis' the proportion is lower—7 per cent of Clark's
subjects (1929), 14 per cent of the Harvard students questioned
by Allport, Gillespie and Young (1948). The rest of the sudden
conversions are those whose interest was set off by an 'emotional
stimulus', but who did not go through a 'definite crisis'.
Perhaps it would be fair to say that between 10 and 30 per cent
of religious people have undergone a more or less violent conversion experience.

The violent conversion experience has been described by the
earlier writers. William James (1902) and other authors have
used literary sources to give examples of famous conversions.
James supported his method by arguing that 'we must make
search rather for the original experiences which were the
pattern-setters to all this mass of suggested feeling and imitated
conduct.' (p. 8). As is pointed out later in this book (p. 143f)
the social learning hypothesis cannot account for such things
as the age of conversion or for other systematic variations of
religious phenomena with empirical variables, although there
is considerable evidence that social learning is *one* factor. The
use of literary sources results in examples of conversion which
are atypical in several ways: (1) these are often conversions of
outstanding religious leaders or were sufficiently extraordinary
to have been placed on record; (2) they were usually sudden,
not gradual conversions, and (3) they were generally conversions of adults, whereas conversion is far more common among
adolescents. It thus appears that literary methods of inquiry
may actually fail to describe the normal as opposed to the
exceptional or pathological phenomenon. Systematic research
can show the frequency of each type of event as well as the
empirical conditions under which each occurs.

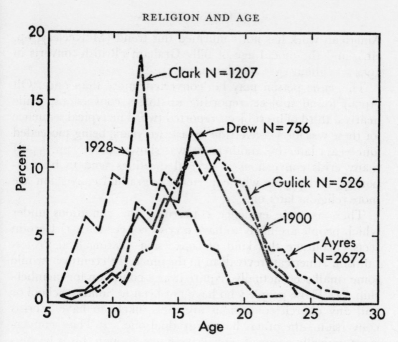

FIGURE 4. The age of conversion
(From Pressey and Kuhlen 1957), by permission of Harper and Bros.

However both approaches agree about the description of the sudden adolescent conversion—a morbid and unrealistic sense of sin and guilt suddenly changes to an ecstatic sense of peace and virtue.

The next problem about conversions is the age at which they occur. The greatest number take place in the sixteenth year for boys, the fifteenth for girls, according to many studies (McKeefery, 1949). Age distributions of several typical investigations are given in Figure 4. It will be seen that the majority fall between 10 and 20, though conversions do occur later; since college students or other young people are often the subjects for these inquiries, later conversions are not reported. Jones (1937) took older people, many of them clergymen, and found some conversions over 40, though these were much less common. Clark (1929) in a careful study of over 2,000 cases, found an average conversion age of 12·8 with a mode at 12, from which some writers have drawn the conclusion that the conversion age had declined since the turn of the century. However, later

American work has not confirmed this trend (McKeefery, op. cit.), and the modal age of Billy Graham's British converts in 1954 was about 15 (Colquhoun, 1955).

The same person may be 'converted' more than once. Olt (1956) found subjects reporting up to six conversions, while nearly a third of his subjects reported two. The typical sequence for these was for a conversion to last two years, being succeeded four years later by another. As was shown above (pp. 54–6) many crisis conversions at revival meetings tend to be temporary, and people who experience a gradual conversion are more religious later on.

There is some evidence concerning the conditions under which people are likely to have a crisis conversion. (1) Certain sects encourage this kind of conversion—Evangelical Protestantism, American revivalism in the nineteenth century—while some small sects actually require it as a condition for membership. (2) Those people who have not been to Sunday School or had any church connexions are more likely to have a crisis conversion—the others have a gradual one. (3) These conversions typically occur at revival meetings, though this is becoming less common. However, about 120,000 people made decisions at Billy Graham's recent campaigns in Great Britain (pp. 53–5).

The relation of the age of conversion to the age of puberty is of some interest in the light of theories relating religion to the sexual instinct. The physical changes comprising puberty may take place at any age between 10 and 17; the distribution is symmetrical and has a peak of 13–13½. Although girls are the first to show the acceleration in growth, the age of first menstruation is slightly later than the corresponding changes in boys. There is some evidence that puberty in girls is now about a year earlier than it was a generation ago (Garrison, 1951). From Figure 4 it seems that about 10 per cent of conversions should take place before puberty—unless those with an early conversion also have an early puberty. Thirty per cent of Starbuck's subjects however (1899) claimed to have been converted *before* puberty, and the distribution curve for conversions shows many conversions after 17.

The foregoing investigations have all been conducted by the questioning of religious people about their experiences during adolescence. The studies now to be discussed compare the average religious activity of different age groups between 10 and 18. An interest in religious and cosmic problems appears at about the age of 12. Associated with an increased intellectual interest in religious affairs comes doubt of what was accepted uncritically earlier. Maclean (1930) found doubts appearing at about the age of 12–13. Hollingworth (1933) found that the awakening of intellectual interest and doubt occurred at a *mental* age of 12, so that more intelligent children start questioning earlier; for example children of IQ 150 come to this stage at the age of 8. Fritsch and Hetzer (1928) studied the diaries of German adolescents and found that doubts were first concerned with church practices and later with the contents of beliefs; this suggests a relation between the growth of doubt and the growth of understanding, since Bose (1929) found that the more abstract religious notions only came to be described correctly towards the end of the period 8–15, while concrete matters of practice—Church festivals and the like—were understood much earlier. Bose found that understanding correlated both with age and IQ (i.e. with mental age), just as Hollingworth found that doubt increased with mental age. Fritsch and Hetzer (1928) found evidence of conflict between an emotional attachment to the religion of childhood and intellectual doubts —faith versus reason—and that this was generally resolved one way or the other by the age of 20, the height of the conflict coming at 17.

Kuhlen and Arnold (1944) surveyed over 500 children grouped around the ages of 12, 15 and 18; the results of this study are given in Table 16. It will be noticed that many specific traditional beliefs are discarded between 12 and 18—for example, 72 per cent of the 12-year-olds believed that 'only good people go to Heaven', as compared with 33 per cent of the 18-year-olds. Beliefs became more abstract and less concrete, and there was more toleration for the ideas of others. There was only a slight increase in the percentages of young people 'wondering about' these topics, though the number reporting definite beliefs declined. The topics most 'wondered about' were Sin, Heaven and Hell, science versus religion, and what happens after death.

Further evidence is provided by a survey of 500 Harvard

TABLE 16. Changes in Specific Religious Beliefs During Adolescence*

Statement	'Believe' per cent			'Wonder about' per cent		
	12 years	15 years	18 years	12 years	15 years	18 years
God is a strange power working for good rather than a person	46	49	57	20	14	15
God is someone who watches you to see that you behave yourself and who punishes you if you are not good	70	49	33	11	13	18
I know there is a God	94	80	79	2	14	16
Catholics, Jews and Protestants are equally good	67	79	86	24	11	7
There is a heaven	82	78	74	13	16	20
Only good people go to heaven	72	45	33	13	27	34
Hell is a place where you are punished for your sins on earth	70	49	35	13	27	34
Heaven is here on earth	12	13	14	18	28	32
People who go to church are better than people who do not go to church	46	26	15	17	21	11
Young people should belong to the same church as their parents	77	56	43	10	11	11
The main reason for going to church is to worship God	88	80	79	4	7	6
It is not necessary to go to church to be a Christian	42	62	67	18	15	8
Only our soul lives after death	72	63	61	18	25	31
Good people say prayers regularly	78	57	47	13	13	27
Prayers are answered	76	69	65	21	25	27
Prayers are a source of help in time of trouble	74	80	83	15	10	9
Prayers are to make up for something that you have done that is wrong	47	24	21	18	17	9
Every word in the Bible is true	79	51	34	15	31	43
It is sinful to doubt the Bible	62	42	27	20	26	28

students by Allport, Gillespie and Young (1948). Asked if they had ever 'reacted either partially or wholly against the beliefs taught', 73 per cent of the Protestants and Jews and 62 per cent

*From Kuhlen and Arnold, 1944, by permission of the Journal Press.

of the Catholics said they had; the median age of rebellion was
15½ for men, 14½ for women. Since the parents would tend on
average to be fairly religious, if these young people were to
rebel at all it would have to be in an irreligious direction: therefore we cannot tell whether the rebellion or the doubt was the
primary factor.

Turning from beliefs to church attendance, several investigators have found a slight decline of interest during the late
teens. Horton (1940) found that this took place during the last
years of High School in America, and before going to college.
Moreton (1944) found a similar decline in England over the
period 15–19. Furthermore, there is no evidence of any increased attendance at any point during the period from 10–
18.

We are now faced with a curious paradox: while the studies
of conversion show a peak of activity at 15–16, the cross-sectional studies show an increasing doubt over the earlier part of
the period, and a decrease of attendance later on. The explanation is quite simple: this period of life is not a time of heightened
activity, as has often been supposed, it is a time of *decision*. The
longitudinal studies of conversion only tell us about those who
decide to become religious. It would be expected that those who
become irreligious make their decision at about the same time.
Since the two sets of decisions take place in opposite directions
simultaneously, both are concealed in the cross-sectional
averages.

YOUNG ADULTHOOD (18–30)

This is a very busy time of life; during this period, many
people leave home, marry, have children and become established in their career. They move from the position of a depen-
dant child to that of an economically responsible adult with
children of his own. What are the religious changes?

The results of several British and American studies are given
in Figure 5. It can be seen that there is a decline from 16–30 on
all criteria of religious activity, and in both countries. Some
surveys of students report that the lowest point is reached at
about 22 (cf. Telford, 1950); it is probably that what is really
appearing here is the decline in religion in the middle of their

college career, which is followed by an increase in their last year (p. 44).

These results are all from recent surveys of cross-sections of the population: are they due to genuine changes with age, or could they be accounted for by historical changes? Assuming that religious attitudes crystallize at about the age of 16, then the present findings could be accounted for by a decline in religion up to 1936, followed by a very sharp revival. Both America and Britain did experience a gradual decline until 1936, but it did not stop there, so the reversal at 30–35 could not be accounted for. There has been a revival in the U.S.A. since about 1945, though in Britain the decline has been continued, yet the pattern is the same in both countries. Again, studies carried out in periods of decline both in Britain (see Figure 5) and in America (Rosander, 1939) all show a falling off in religious activity between 18 and 30. We may conclude fairly confidently that the decline between 18 and 30 is genuine and not due to historical factors.

Although there is a lapse from religion on average, it must be remembered that some people have their first or subsequent conversions during this time. Something like 40 per cent of Billy Graham's London converts were aged 19 or over (Colquhoun, 1955) though 15 per cent is a more usual figure, as Figure 4 shows. Some people may encounter environmental pressures towards religion when they go to college during the 19–21 period (p. 42f).

Little mention has been made of mystical experience in this book, simply because of the lack of statistical evidence about it. The earlier writers like William James (1902) observe that mystical experiences often occur during and after adolescent conversion. Pratt (1924), while quoting no statistics, suggests on the basis of extensive literary and other evidence that the height of these experiences comes normally at about 22, and fades away between 25 and 30.

The decline in religious activity between 18 and 30 is an important and little-known phenomenon. There may be some who in the enthusiasm of adolescence and the social pressures of college become ordained, and even enter the Mission Field, to regret it later. Perhaps this phenomenon is implicitly recognized by the monastic orders of the Church of England, in

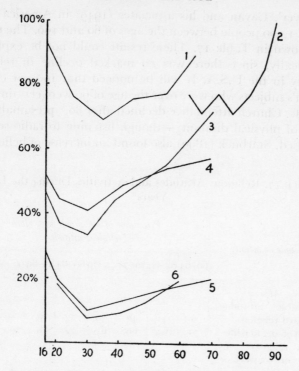

FIGURE 5. Changes in religious activity between the
ages 16–90

Key
1. Attendance at weekly Mass—Catholics (Fichter 1952)—
   U.S.A.
2. Certain of an after-life (Cavan *et al.*, 1949)—U.S.A.
3. Daily prayer (Gorer 1955)—G.B.
4. Believe in after-life (loc. cit.).
5. Weekly attendance (loc. cit.).
6. Weekly attendance (Cauter & Downham 1954)—G.B.

which it is not possible to take final vows before the age of
30.

LATER ADULTHOOD (30 ONWARDS)

From the age of 30, there is a steady increase in religious
activity. This is shown by the results which are plotted in
Figure 5, showing an increase of activity and belief up to '90

and over'. Cavan and his associates (1949) in America questioned 1,200 people between the ages of 60 and 100. The results are shown in Table 17. These results could not be explained historically, since there was no marked decline in religious activity in the U.S.A. It will be noticed that 100 per cent of Cavan's subjects who were over the age of 90 were certain of the afterlife. Church attendance declined after 80—presumably because of physical disability—though listening to radio services increased. Starbuck (1899) also found an increase of belief with

TABLE 17. Religious Attitudes and Activities During the Later Years*

Attitude or activity	Percentage of age group with given religious attitude							
	60–64	65–69	70–74	75–79	80–84	85–89	90–94	95–99
Men								
Favourable attitudes toward religion	38	41	42	39	53	55	50	
Certain of an after-life	71	64	69	67	72	81	100	100
Attend religious services once a week or oftener	45	41	46	45	50	45	17	
Listen to church services regularly on radio	16	21	19	26	33	37	20	50
Read Bible at least once a week	25	29	33	41	48	45	33	25
Women								
Favourable attitudes toward religion	51	56	57	64	69	81	93	100
Certain of an after-life	83	78	86	77	91	90	100	100
Attend religious services once a week or oftener	60	53	52	53	56	33	50	
Listen to church services regularly on radio	22	27	37	30	46	59	69	100
Read Bible at least once a week	50	60	64	62	61	76	58	100

*From Cavan, R. S., *et al.* 1949.

age; he found that the nature of the beliefs changed—belief in God and the after-life increased, but belief in specific Christian dogmas declined. Kingsbury (1937) also found qualitative changes with age. Reasons given for going to church changed markedly; after 30 the number saying 'habit', 'to encourage family attendance', 'to keep alive the spirit of Christ' and 'for reassurance of immortality' increased rapidly—the last two to 80 per cent at 50 plus. Other reasons given fell off with age—such as 'to formulate a philosophy of life', 'to gain new friends' and 'to hear literature and music'.

The heightened religion of age is very different from the heightened religion of adolescence. In adolescence there is a great intellectual perplexity and doubt coupled with emotional turmoil: young people suddenly change their whole orientation one way or the other. In old age, when both intellect and emotions are dimmed, there is no worry about the niceties of theology, nor is there any emotional excitement about religious matters: old people increasingly take part in religious practices which have long been habitual, and in belief are primarily concerned with the central facts of God and the after-life.

Ordinary conversions are rare after 30. However, those rare but important events, sometimes known as 'mystical conversions' (Thouless, 1924), do occur during this period. By a mystical conversion is meant the occasion on which an already religious person begins to have emotional religious experiences of a stronger and more continuous nature, and which may lead to his taking up a contemplative life. Bucke (1901) describes forty-three such cases including some of the famous historical saints and mystics. Almost all of them had their mystical conversion in the thirties, often at about the age of 33. This is clearly a quite different affair from adolescent conversion, and Thouless suggests a different explanation for it (1924).

Summary for Chapter 6 (3–10). Children are considerably religious, at first holding fairy-tale beliefs, later accepting the standard ideas of their group. (10–18) Intellectual doubts start at a mental age of 12, followed by emotional stress; these conflicts are often resolved at about the age of 16 either by conversion to religion or by a decision to abandon the religion of childhood. About 20 per cent of those converted towards religion experience a sudden crisis, the rest are 'graduals'. There is no general increase in religious activity during these years. (18–30) There is a sharp decline in all aspects of religious activity, the years 30–35 being the lowest point in the life-cycle. (35 onwards) There is a steady increase from about 35 until old age, which is marked by widespread belief in God and the after-life.

Explanation. The religious interest of children may be explained by theories relating the Heavenly Family to the human family (pp. 161–4). Conflicts in adolescence may be due to differing environmental pressures, as may gradual conversion in either direction (pp. 143–5). Sudden conversions may be the result of the sudden acceptance of salvationist beliefs by adolescents with guilt-feelings over sex (p. 160). The heightened religion of age may be due to anxiety about the hereafter (pp. 152–3). The inactivity of 30–35 could be explained negatively, by saying that neither the mechanisms of adolescence nor those of age are operative. It could also be suggested that this is a time of life when people are much occupied with their children and careers and are temporarily drawn away from religious interests.

VII

SEX DIFFERENCES

THE differences between men and women in their religious behaviour and beliefs are considerable. Furthermore, since many social surveys report the results for the two sexes separately, there is a lot of evidence available. This is therefore one of the most important of the statistical comparisons to be made in this book. We shall first consider the extent of the difference, using various criteria for religious activity, and go on to compare different denominations for the proportion of male and female members.

SEX DIFFERENCES ON DIFFERENT CRITERIA

The percentages of men and women who engage in various kinds of religious behaviour are given in the tables. It is obvious that women are more religious on every criterion. It is possible to derive various indices of *how much* more religious they are. The index which we shall use is the *ratio* of the percentage of women to the percentage of men who engage in the activity in question. The main difficulty with this index is that it is smaller when both percentages are large. Since Americans are rather more religious on most criteria than English people, it is not possible to compare English and American sex ratios, and so they will be treated separately.

Church attendance statistics are shown in Table 18. The four British surveys give very consistent results, apart from a slightly different figure for the town of Derby. A representative figure for the ratio of the two percentages is 1·5, i.e. 50 per cent more women than men go to church once a week on average. Of the American surveys, the two Gallup polls reached the most representative sample; the sharp increase between 1950 and 1954 is shown clearly here. A representative value for the ratio here would be 1·25—i.e. 25 per cent more American women go to

71

church once a week. As argued above, the difference between the British and American indices is simply an artefact: if the percentages of English men and women who go to church at least once every three months are compared we get 44 and 55 per cent—giving an index of 1·25 which is the same as the American figure (Odham, 1947).

TABLE 18. Sex Differences in Weekly Church Attendance

GREAT BRITAIN

Author or organization	Population surveyed	Percentage of Men	Women	Ratio
B.I.P.O. (Gorer 1955, p. 271)	British Adults 1948	12	18	1·5
Odham (1947)	English adults 1947	10·7	17·7	1·65
Cauter and Downham (1954)	Sample of 1,200 in Derby	11	15	1·36
B.I.P.O. (Gregory 1957)	British adults 1957	11	17	1·55

U.S.A.

Author or organization	Population surveyed	Percentage of Men	Women	Ratio
Gallup Poll (Rosten 1955, p. 241)	Adult population 1950	34	44	1·29
Gallup Poll (Rosten 1955, p. 241)	Adult population 1954	42	50	1·19
A.I.P.O. (Cantril 1951, p. 699)	High School students 1942	49·6	63·5	1·28
Ross (1950)	1,935 Y.M.C.A. members	45·3	57·3	1·26
Allport et al. (1948)	Harvard and Radcliffe students	25	39	1·56

Beliefs, in God and the after-life for example, also vary between the sexes. Table 19 summarizes the findings in this area. Of the British surveys, the Mass Observation results are not very reliable, since they are not based upon a proper sample. The American results show considerable variety in the percentages shown; this is a result of variations in the wording of the question, and of the age of the people questioned. Representative figures for the ratio of percentages are 1·4 for Britain (belief in after-life) and 1·1 for the U.S.A. These results are supported by the findings of several studies which showed that women were more conservative in belief than men.

The saying of private prayers daily, together with allied activities such as reading the Bible at home, has been surveyed by a number of investigators. Table 20 shows the main results. The four surveys carried out in Great Britain are consistent in giving a percentage ratio of about 1·65—the Cauter and Downham survey of Derby was very carefully conducted, and should be

TABLE 19. Sex Differences in Beliefs
GREAT BRITAIN

		Percentages of		
		Men	Women	Ratio
Belief in an After-life				
Gorer (op. cit.)		39	56	1·44
Mass Observation				
(1947)	London suburb 1945–6	36	52	1·44
Belief in God				
Mass Observation (op. cit.)		66	80	1·21

U.S.A.

		Men	Women	Ratio
Belief in an After-life				
Gallup Poll (Rosten op. cit., p. 238)		73	79	1·08
Allport *et al.* (op. cit.)		41	43	1·05
Belief in God				
Gallup Poll (Rosten op. cit., p. 237)		95	97	1·02
Ross (op. cit.)		70·4	81·6	1·16
Katz and Allport (1931)	1,502 liberal art students	63	74	1·17
Allport *et al.* (op. cit.)		62	66	1·06

TABLE 20. Sex Differences in Saying Private Prayers
GREAT BRITAIN

		Percentages of		
		Men	Women	Ratio
B.I.P.O.	British adults 1950 (Do you, personally, believe in prayer?)	57	80	1·40
Gorer (op. cit.)	(Say private prayers daily)	31	58	1·87
Cauter & Downham (op. cit.)	(Read Bible frequently)	8	13	1·63
Mass Observation (op. cit.)	(Pray outside church)	43	78	1·81

U.S.A.

		Men	Women	Ratio
Ross (op. cit)	(Prayers daily)	37·8	64·2	1·70
Allport *et al.* (op. cit.)	(Prayers daily)	22	35	1·59

weighted accordingly. Ross's study of Y.M.C.A. members in America gives the very similar figure of 1·70, and Allport's study of Harvard students gives 1·59.

Church membership is a useful criterion which will be made the basis for denominational comparisons later. The percentages ratio for American church members can be calculated in two ways. In the 1936 Census of Religious Bodies (*Census*, 1936) the total membership of men and women is given as 20·13 million and 25·65 million respectively. This gives a percentage ratio of 1·32.* However, if we compare the percentages of people claiming to be church members in social surveys, a ratio of about 1·10 is obtained (cf. Rosten, op. cit., p. 239). This is partly an artefact resulting from the higher percentages of claimed members, but it must also be the case that a lot of men claim to be members who are not.

No comparable figures are available from British records, but the surveys by Gorer and the B.I.P.O. found that about 80–90 per cent of the population claim affiliation, with a sex ratio of about 1·08—similar to the American ratio of 1·10 for reported membership.

Attitudes towards the Church and towards religion also vary between the sexes. The Thurstone–Chave scale of attitudes towards the Church was used by Newcomb and Svehla (1937), who found women consistently more favourable; the difference was greatest for working class subjects and for young people. Several other investigators obtained the same result, but Gilliland (1953) found no sex differences among students on this measure or on Thurstone scales for attitudes towards the Reality of God and Influence on Conduct. Spoerl (1952) and others have found that women score higher than men on the religious value of the Vernon–Allport scale; they also score higher on the aesthetic and social values. Kirkpatrick (1949) similarly found that women were high on both 'religionism' and humanitarianism than men, and that the correlation between these dimensions was higher for women. Terman and Miles (1936) found considerable differences between the sexes in the amount of interest expressed in religion, so that those of each sex who were

---

*After making allowance for the fact that there were 0·7 per cent more men in the population. (*Census* 1940.)

interested scored high on the dimension of 'femininity'. Lenski
(1953) similarly found that 66 per cent more women than men
expressed 'much' interest in religion. Finally it should be mentioned that Sinclair (1928) found that 76 per cent of his subjects
who had mystical experiences were women, 72 per cent of his
extreme non-mystics were men.

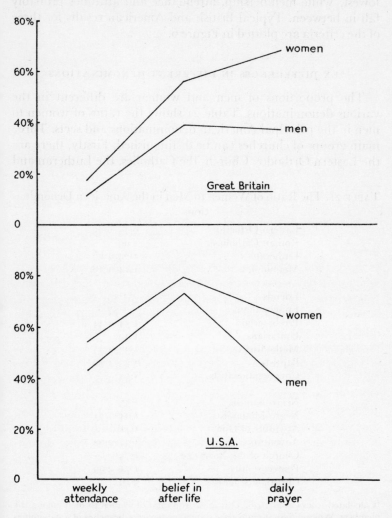

FIGURE 6. Sex differences on three criteria for G.B. and U.S.A.

The sex differences on a number of criteria have now been established. It is difficult to compare these results, since the index diminishes with the size of the percentages involved, but some allowance can be made for this. The most striking result is that the ratio for private prayer is larger than for any other criterion—about 1·65. The ratio for beliefs appears to be the lowest, while membership, attendance and attitudes probably fall in between. Typical British and American results for three of the criteria are plotted in Figure 6.

SEX DIFFERENCES IN DIFFERENT DENOMINATIONS

The proportions of men and women are different in the various denominations. Table 21 shows the ratios of women to men in the principal American denominations and sects. Three main groups of churches can be distinguished. Firstly, there are the Eastern Orthodox Church, the Catholics, the Lutheran and

TABLE 21. The Ratio of Women to Men in the American Denominations

Eastern Orthodox	0·75–0·99
Roman Catholics	1·09
Lutherans	1·04–1·23
Mennonites	1·14–1·16
Friends	1·25
Episcopalians	1·37
Presbyterians	1·34–1·44
Unitarians	1·40
Methodists	1·33–1·47
Baptists	1·35–1·50
Congregationalists	1·55
Negro Baptists	1·55
Negro Methodists	1·64–1·71
Assembly of God	1·71
Adventists	1·52–2·00
Church of the Nazarene	1·75
Pentecostalists	1·71–2·09
Christian Scientists	3·19

(Calculated from *Census* 1936. This shows the ratio of women to men among the members. When different figures are shown for separate branches of a denomination, the range of ratios for the main branches is given)

the Mennonite churches—with up to 15 per cent more women than men, and with more men than women in some cases. Secondly there are the major Protestant bodies which have between 25 and 55 per cent more women. Thirdly, the Pentecostal Church and similar minor Protestant sects have over 55 per cent more women. The above classification can be summarized by saying that the proportion of women is higher the further one moves towards extreme Protestantism.

Figures for the Jews are not given in the Census of Religious Bodies (1936), but other evidence suggests that Jewish women are in fact less religious than the men. Katz and Allport (1931) found the Jewish women students less favourable towards the church than were the men, and Nathan (1932) and Woolston (1937) found fewer Jewish women with orthodox beliefs among large samples of students. This was not confirmed by Franzblau (1934) for schoolchildren, and it may be the case that Jewish women do not go to college so frequently if they are religious.

The ratio for Catholics can be analysed in greater detail on the basis of figures obtained by Fichter (1952) for three Catholic parishes, involving 8,363 people. The differences are greatest for Confession, especially for older people, where the ratio is 1·93. For the obligatory functions of Easter duties and Mass, which over 80 per cent attended, the sex differences were slight. This supports Katz and Allport's suggestion (1931) that the sex ratio is smaller the greater the institutional pressure to conform. This fits in also with the greater sex differences found on private prayer compared with attendance at church services.

The major Protestant denominations have a somewhat higher proportion of women than the Catholic church. As shown in Table 21, there are 25 to 55 per cent more women members for these denominations in America. Rowntree and Lavers (1951) counted attendance in York and found 57 per cent more women in Nonconformist churches, 48 per cent more in the Church of England and 23 per cent more in the Roman Catholic churches.*

The minor Protestant sects have much the highest ratio; Table 21 shows that in America there are over 55 per cent more women members. The highest ratio of all is found for the

*However, Mudie-Smith (1904) reporting an earlier count of attendances in London obtained the corresponding figures of 17, 57 and 35 per cent.

Christian Scientists, who have more than three women to each male member. Wilson (1955) in his study of English small sects found a ratio of 2–3 : 1 for attendance at the Elim Foursquare Gospel, 2–4 : 1 for the Christian Scientists, but only about 1·25 : 1 for the Christadelphians: Wilson accounts for the small ratio for this latter sect by the lack of emotional release at the services. Farr and Howe (1932) found a ratio of 1·8 : 1 for mental patients belonging to the main Protestant sects, and 4 : 1 for those belonging to small sects. It might be expected that women would experience sudden conversions more often, but this is not always the case. McKeefery (1949) summarizes his own and several earlier American studies; in each case a slightly higher percentage of men report sudden conversions. However, in Billy Graham's campaign in Glasgow the ratio for converts was about 1·8 : 1 (Colquhoun, 1955).

Finally it should be noted that the Negro churches in America have a higher proportion of female members than the corresponding white denominations. In Table 21 it can be seen that the Negro Methodists and Baptists have a rather higher ratio than the main Methodist and Baptist churches, and this is also true for Lutherans.

Summary for Chapter 7. Women are more religious than men on all criteria, particularly for private prayer, also for membership, attendance and attitudes, while differences in belief are small. This sex difference varies between denominations, the minor sects having most women, followed by the major Protestant denominations; there are about as many men as women in Catholic and Orthodox bodies.

Direction of Causation. Since a person's sex is constant, this, or factors associated with it, must be the causal variable here. Different theories to explain sex differences posit as the cause different sociological or psychological factors connected with sex differences.

Explanation. Many theories have been or could be suggested to account for the fact that women are more religious than men. The problem is to decide which is correct, and this can only be done by deducing further predictions from the theories, which can be tested. From the discussion of theories given later, two

78

possible explanations for this result emerge. (*a*) If the function of religion is to relieve guilt feelings, and if women have more guilt feelings than men, women should be more religious (pp. 158–60). In fact women do have more guilt feelings; furthermore the proportion of women rises as we move from Catholicism towards extreme Protestantism, as would be expected from the emphasis on sin and salvation in the latter groups; data on suicide and crime also support the theory (pp. 157–8). (*b*) If God is a projected father figure, as Freud suggests, and if children prefer the opposite-sex parent, it follows that girls should be more concerned with a deity presented as a fatherly male (pp. 161–4). This theory too can explain denominational differences: Catholicism offers a mother-figure in the Virgin Mary, so that this faith should be as attractive to men as to women, whereas Protestantism should not be.

Can a crucial test be made of these two explanations? The first theory predicts that women would engage even more in private prayer, since they are motivated by internalized processes, while men, as authoritarians, are religious as a result of external sanctions: this result is obtained, and cannot be accounted for on the second theory. Furthermore, the second theory has a weak link: the postulate that children prefer the opposite-sex parent has never been confirmed, preferences being apparently independent of sex (Sears, 1943).

VIII

INDIVIDUAL DIFFERENCES IN PERSONALITY TRAITS AND ATTITUDES

THERE are differences in religious belief and behaviour between people who have been subjected to similar environmental influences of the kind described earlier, and who are of the same age, sex and social class. These differences are found to be associated with certain personality variables and must either be caused by these or be influenced by some of the factors producing the traits.

There are hundreds of personality variables which have been measured by psychologists. Some of these have become the object of much more attention than others: these are the ones which have been found to have internal consistency when measured in a variety of ways, as can be shown for example by factor analysis. To know a person's score along one of these dimensions is to be able to predict his behaviour in many situations. In the case of attitudes another criterion is the interest attached to the attitude itself—*political* and *racial* attitudes being of great intrinsic interest. Some attitudes and traits are of particular importance for our present purpose because they show high and consistent correlations with religious beliefs and behaviour. The dimensions included are the two attitudes mentioned above, the two personality traits of *authoritarianism* and *suggestibility*, and the dimension of *intelligence*. There is no special section on motivation since measurements are as yet unsatisfactory, though some findings on the *achievement motive* are included in the section on intelligence.

Variations in personality are partly the result of inheritance

---

Note. Summaries are given at the end of each section in this chapter.

which shows itself also in the relation between personality and physical constitution. It is quite likely that there is some relationship between physique and religious beliefs—as put forward by Aldous Huxley in *Eyeless in Gaza*; Coffin (1944) did in fact find a correlation of a ·38 between scores on the religious value on the Vernon–Allport scale and self-ratings of 'Ectomorphy', i.e. being thin and linear in physique, in an exploratory study of 156 students. It might be expected that there would be some direct inheritance of religious beliefs via these personality characteristics, but this has never been investigated. Probably some of the parent-child similarity in religious activity is the result of such genetic factors. Personality is also influenced by the socialization process during childhood, different stages being stressed by different groups of psychologists. It would follow that religious beliefs should be associated directly with particular styles of upbringing, and some evidence that that is the case was given earlier (p. 42).

POLITICAL ATTITUDES

Political attitudes may be defined by the way a person votes or says he votes. Alternatively, attitude scales can be constructed which differentiate between Radicals and Conservatives—they include items on such subjects as private enterprise and economic security.

Religious people are more conservative in politics than nonreligious people. Table 22 gives the results of a British survey and shows the very low percentage of people with no religion who vote conservative.

TABLE 22. Denomination and Voting, Great Britain 1951

	Conservative	Labour	Liberal
C. of E.	45	37	8
Noncon.	27·5	40·5	18
R.C.	33	51	6
Scottish Church	43·5	37	7·5
Other	33	35·5	15
None	17	54	6

(From Eysenck 1954, p. 21)

British and American surveys show that Protestants tend to vote Conservative more than Catholics, and that Jews support left-wing parties: Centers (1951) found a correlation of ·36 between Protestantism and church membership in America. This is probably partly due to class differences, since Catholics have a higher working class composition in both countries. However, a number of American studies show that Protestants are still more Republican with social class held constant (cf. Lipset *et al.*, 1954, p. 1140). Table 23 shows this for Lazarfeld's study (1944) of Erie County.

TABLE 23. Denomination, Voting and Social Class, Erie County
1944

	Protestant	Catholic
Av+	76	29
Av	66	25
Av−	54	23
Very poor	43	14

(Percentage of the denomination voting republican; from Lazarsfeld 1944)

Centers (op. cit.) found a correlation of ·36 between Protestantism and republican voting, and ·19 between Protestantism and social class—showing that class differences between denominations are only a partial explanation.

These results using voting as a criterion of political attitude are paralleled by investigations using attitude scales—where radical opinions are generally defined as those favouring communism and birth control and being opposed to war. Such studies agree with the others in finding that religious people are more conservative (e.g. Carlson, 1934). However, it has been found in a number of American studies that Catholics* hold more conservative attitudes than Protestants, and Protestants than Jews (Sappenfield, 1942), although the voting statistics show Protestants as most conservative. The explanation may be that Catholics vote democrat as the result of an historical tradition: the Irish and German immigrants in the second half of the last century settled in the cities and the Democratic party was favourably inclined towards them, as well as having more influence among the urban population. (Lubell, 1956.) English Catholics similarly contain many Irish who are traditionally

*It should be noted that these scales include items on sexual ethics and other matters on which Catholic teaching is 'conservative'; items on drinking and gambling might produce different results (Nowlan, 1957).

opposed to the Tories. Lipset (op. cit, p. 1140) shows that members of religious minority groups often support left-wing parties. It seems likely that Catholics have an intrinsically right wing attitude, but they may vote for left-wing parties in America and Great Britain for one of the reasons mentioned. Jews have left-wing votes and attitudes, and in America this is quite inconsistent with their class position.

Finally there is some evidence that religious people are less interested in politics. Ringer and Glock (1955) found that parishioners most committed to the church were least willing to allow the priest to participate in politics. Similar findings are reported later on the relation between religious activity and concern over social issues. Part of the explanation may lie in the inverse pattern of relations between religious and political interests and the age-sex variables: women are more concerned with religion, men with politics; young and old people are most active in religion, the age group 35–55 in politics (Lipset, loc. cit.).

Summary. Religious people are more conservative and are less interested in politics than other people. Catholics have more conservative attitudes, but in Britain and America support left-wing parties: this is partly due to class differences. Protestants support right-wing parties, Jews support the left and have radical attitudes.

Explanation. See p. 92.

RACIAL PREJUDICE

Several American surveys have found that religious people are more prejudiced against Jews and negroes, as shown by attitude scales on racial attitudes. Table 24 shows the scores on scales of ethnocentrism for 1,332 people studied in the 'Authoritarian personality' investigations in California.

Some investigators have not obtained these results. Chein for instance found a correlation between prejudice and church attendance, but when he analysed denominations separately the correlation was reversed; his Catholics were more prejudiced than his Protestants, the Protestants than the Jews, and since the Catholics attended church more often, this created a

TABLE 24. Ethnocentrism and Religion

Catholics	4·21
Major Prot. Denom.	3·89
Minor Prot. Sects	2·49 (n=23)
Unitarians	1·99 (n=23)
No denom.	2·71
Church attenders	3·96
Non-attenders	2·87
Religion important	180·7
Religion unimportant	115·4

(From Adorno *et al.* (1950), pp. 210–17)

spurious overall correlation between attendance and prejudice (cf. Harding, *et al.*, 1954, p. 1039). Similarly, Prothro and Jensen (1950) found small positive correlations of ·05 and ·09 between favourable attitudes to the church and towards Negroes and Jews respectively; correlations were computed separately for six colleges which were denominationally fairly pure. Parry (1949) found that non church-going Protestants were more prejudiced than church-going Protestants, and Allport (1954) found less prejudice in a group of twenty fervent Catholics than in twenty 'who seemed more influenced by the political and social aspects of religious activity' (p. 452). However many investigations show that atheists and agnostics are less prejudiced—this is shown in Table 24 and was found in Ross's study (1950) of 2,000 Y.M.C.A. members. It seems possible that there may be a curvilinear relation between religious activity and prejudice: out-and-out atheists and agnostics are less prejudiced than church members who never go to church, while more frequent attenders are also less prejudiced. It is not the genuinely devout who are prejudiced but the conventionally religious.

Turning now to denominational differences, it has often been found that Catholics are the most prejudiced, members of the major Protestant bodies slightly less so. This was found in the Authoritarian Personality research, where it also emerged that members of small sects were very low in prejudice, though only twenty-three such people were tested. Chein, as reported above, found Catholics, Protestants and Jews to be prejudiced in that

order, while Allport and Kramer (1946) in a study of 437
students found 71 per cent of Catholics in the most prejudiced
half, compared with 62 per cent of Protestants, 22 per cent of
Jews and 27 per cent of those with no religious upbringing. It
will be noticed that the Catholic-Protestant difference is slight,
and it has occasionally been found that Catholics are *less* prejudiced (cf. Harding, *et al*, 1954). Spoerl (1951) and Parry
(1949) found that members of different denominations were
prejudiced towards different groups: generally speaking
Catholics are prejudiced towards negroes and orientals, Protestants towards Jews and working class minority groups, while
Jews are prejudiced towards white majority groups.

Although there is evidence that members of the Catholic
church in America tend to be slightly more prejudiced than
other people, it should be noted that the leaders of this church
have been prominent in opposing racial segregation both in the
U.S.A. and in South Africa.

Summary. Regular and devout church attenders tend to be
less prejudiced than non-attending members, though religious
people in general are more prejudiced than non-religious
people. Catholics are most prejudiced, closely followed by the
major Protestant denominations; Jews and sect members are the
least prejudiced.

Explanation. See p. 91–2.

SUGGESTIBILITY

As several investigations have now shown, suggestibliity
is not a single trait, but is composed of a number of relatively independent elements. Eysenck (1947) experimented
with a variety of different test situations and concluded that
there were at least three types—(1) Primary (or psychomotor)
suggestibility, in which people carry out a motor movement,
upon repeated suggestion by the experimenter but without
conscious participation by the agent, (2) Secondary suggestibility, in which people will perceive or remember the thing
suggested, and (3) Prestige suggestion, in which people change
their opinion after being told that a prestige person holds a
different one.

There is considerable evidence that religious conservatives are high on prestige suggestibility. Symington (1935) studied 612 people using a comprehensive test of orthodoxy of belief. There was clear evidence from the questionnaire answers that the conservatives were more dependent on group opinion—for example the liberals reported that they disliked being told what to do, and gave evidence of facing the facts squarely before forming an opinion. Dreger (1952) studied thirty people from each extreme of liberalism and conservativism out of an initial group of 490, the groups being carefully equated for other variables. Various scores from the Thematic Apperception Test and the Rorschach indicated that conservatives had a greater need for dependence than the liberals. Finally the fact that authoritarians are more religious, combined with Hoffman's finding (1953) that they are more affected by social influence, points to the same conclusion.

Supplementary evidence comes from investigations of self-confidence and inferiority feelings. Janis (1954) found that subjects who were low on ratings of self-esteem—including depression and inhibition of aggression—were more influenced by written propaganda. Neurotic, particularly obsessional, people were less influenced. A number of studies show that Catholics and other religious conservatives are lacking in self-confidence and self-esteem. Symington's conservatives (1935) considered that there were more things wrong with them on the Pressey test. Several studies of Catholic theological students and novices show them to be submissive and to have inferiority feelings on various personality tests or self-ratings (e.g. McCarthy, 1942).

There is evidence on primary suggestibility from a variety of religious groups, in every case showing that religious people are more suggestible in this sense too. Howells (1928) gave a series of psychomotor tests to fifty extreme radicals and the same number of conservatives. Five tests of psychomotor suggestibility all showed the conservatives to be the more suggestible. Sinclair (1928) obtained similar results comparing fifty students who did have marked mystical experiences with fifty at the other extreme. Primary suggestibility seems to be particularly strong amongst members of revivalist and evangelical bodies. As reported in another section (pp. 52–53), many people at early revivals showed signs of twitching and jerking

86

before finally collapsing; this is primary suggestibility and may be a particular trait of revivalist audiences. Some of them go to hospital in states of 'religious excitement', a form of hysteria (p. 106). Coe (1916) studied 100 people who had been converted, and found that those who had been converted 'suddenly', i.e. at revivals, produced motor automatisms more frequently under hypnosis. Brown and Lowe (1951) tested a large number of students on the Minnesota Multiphasic Personality Inventory (MMPI) and found that a group of Bible students—who would be extreme Protestants—scored high on hysteria. Janet and others thought that hysterics were particularly prone to primary suggestibility. Eysenck (1947) found that while neurotics in general were thus suggestible, hysterics were no more so than other neurotics; however, he agrees that the impersonal suggestions which were used might have been less effective for hysterics than face-to-face suggestions (p. 190).

Summary. Religious conservatives are subject to prestige suggestion. Various religious groups have been found to be high on primary suggestibility, but this is probably most true of extreme Protestants.

AUTHORITARIANISM

A number of investigators have drawn up questionnaires containing miscellaneous political, religious and other items, and have studied the statistical relations between these items. In particular they have arrived at two or more 'factors' which between them will stand for the original items, and from which an individual's score on any particular item can be predicted. Ferguson (1944) did a series of such factor analyses, and one of his factors he called 'humanitarianism': this was measured by scales measuring attitudes towards war, capital punishment and the treatment of criminals—these three correlating closely with one another. His second factor was called 'religionism', which will be discussed later.

The next study to be considered is that of Adorno and others (1950) on the Authoritarian Personality, which was mentioned above in connexion with racial prejudice. Attitude scales were developed for Anti-Semitism, Ethnocentrism and for Political and Economic Conservatism: these correlated to the extent of ·43–·76. From these a further scale, the F-scale, was developed which would measure the basic personality mechanisms underlying the previous tendencies without referring directly to them. This scale correlated with the others to the extent of ·53–·73 and was taken as a measure of 'authoritarianism'. There has been a lot of research on this dimension and it is now clear that it is by no means a pure factor, but rather a combination of several tendencies. The F-scale measures the opposite of Ferguson's humanitarianism (Eysenck, 1954, p. 238), as can be seen by comparison of the items in the two scales.

Eysenck (1944) factor analysed 700 replies to a thirty-two-item questionnaire. As shown in Figure 7, he obtained factors of Radicalism-Conservativism and of tough and tender mindedness. Inspection of the items in the various quadrants however shows that the fourth quadrant contains the orthodox conserva-

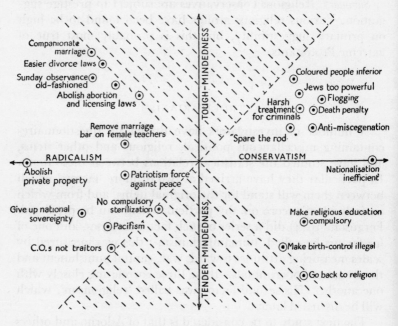

FIGURE 7. Eysenck's R and T factors.

(From Eysenck 1953, p. 229; by permission of Professor Eysenck)

tive religious views corresponding to Ferguson's religionism factor, while the second quadrant contains items on evolution and sex representing the opposite pole of the religionism factor. Similarly, the first and third quadrants correspond to humanitarianism. As Eysenck says, 'when the results . . . are compared with Ferguson's analysis, it will be found that agreement is striking with respect to the actual position of the items, but that his two main factors . . . are rotated from R(adicalism) and T(ough-minded) through an angle of 45°. (1953, p. 233.)

In Eysenck's and Ferguson's analyses, religionism and authoritarianism (or humanitarianism) are shown at right angles—i.e. as statistically independent. However, as shown previously (p. 84) authoritarianism is considerably higher for religious people, and in particular for Catholics, though certain Protestant sects are low on it. Similarly, Kirkpatrick (1949) made a careful study of the correlation between religionism and humanitarianism, including an analysis of a stratified sample of 215 individuals, and found a correlation of —·24. Such variations in the results are presumably due to different definitions of the dimensions being considered. The general relations between authoritarianism, political conservativism and religionism may be represented as in Figure 8.

If *authoritarianism* is measured in a way which makes it more like political conservatism, then there is a closer correlation with religion. If *religionism* is defined in a way which stresses orthodoxy of belief and church membership rather than church attendance, it will lie in the 'A' position in Figure 8, and be associated with authoritarianism, political conservatism and prejudice. If religionism is defined by church attendance and other measures of genuine religious involvement, it will lie in position 'B', and may be associated with low race prejudice, liberal rather than conservative views in politics, and low scores on authoritarianism. Religionism A is stronger for Catholics and other religious conservatives, Religionism B for Unitarians, Jews and other religious liberals. This fits in with the fact that Catholics are higher on authoritarianism than Protestants, and Protestants higher than Jews (p. 84; Lipset, 1953).

Another phase of the Adorno project studied the personality variables associated with authoritarianism. The results of a series of clinical interviews with people at the extremes of the

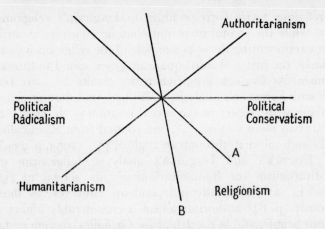

FIGURE 8. Religion and Authoritarianism

dimension show that authoritarians (i) have greater repression of unacceptable tendencies in themselves, (ii) project these impulses on to others, who may be seen as hostile and threatening, (iii) show a higher degree of conformity, (iv) are more concerned with power than love in dealings with other people and (v) have a rigid kind of personality. The tendency of authoritarians to use projection (ii) as a defence mechanism will be referred to in the theoretical section of the book. Their conformity and tendency to submit to social pressures (iii) will be used to account for the hierarchical structure of the Catholic church.

A related personality variable is that of punitiveness: people are said to be extrapunitive if they react to frustration by aggression directed outwards, intropunitive if the aggression is directed inwards, and impunitive if they do not react aggressively at all. This aspect of personality is often measured by means of the Rosenzweig Picture-Frustration test (1946), a projection test in which reactions to various forms of frustration are expressed: the test has been found to correlate with overt measures of aggression. It would be expected that authoritarians would be extrapunitive, in view of their hostility towards out-groups and their weak internalization of a super-ego (pp. 159–60). Sanford (1950) gave tests for both dimensions to 1,000 subjects and found that the authoritarians reacted

90

extrapunitively unless the frustrating person was powerful, in which case they were intropunitive; the humanitarians on the other hand responded impunitively, King and Funkenstein (1957) found that religious conservatives and those whose fathers were stern disciplinarians (two correlates of authoritarianism) had the same cardiovascular stress reaction that is found when anger is directed outwards.

Summary. Authoritarianism is higher for religious people in general, particularly for Catholics and other religious conservatives, though it is probably low for Unitarians, Jews and members of minor sects.

Explanation of the findings on political attitudes, prejudice, suggestibility and authoritarianism. Authoritarianism is a very important dimension of personality because it is highly correlated with many other personality variables (Titus and Hollander, 1957), and because something is known about the dynamic mechanisms underlying it (Adorno *et al.*, 1950); it will be used here to account for the findings of the three previous sections.

The theory that God is a projection of the super-ego resulting from conflict with the instincts applies particularly to authoritarians: since they use projection as a defence mechanism they believe in a powerful, forbidding God, while because they prefer hierarchical organizations and are willing to accept social pressures they find the Roman Catholic and similar churches congenial (p. 159). It is probable that hierarchical churches encourage authoritarian tendencies and that certain methods of child-rearing are perpetuated in the Catholic sub-culture, so that both directions of causation are operative.

The higher racial prejudice of religious people, especially of Catholics, would be expected in view of the close connexion between authoritarianism and prejudice; the explanation of this connexion is that authoritarians are extrapunitive, and tend to repress unacceptable tendencies in themselves and to project them on to others. The finding that devout people are *less* prejudiced than conventional church members is particularly interesting; Adorno and others (1950) found that the religion of authoritarians was indeed more superficial and conventional than that of humanitarians, who were more inwardly involved—though there was a strong statistical tendency for more authoritarians to be church-goers and members. Clearly the devout and less prejudiced are religious as a result of other psychological mechanisms—possibly through reduction of guilt feelings (pp. 155-6).

Authoritarians are conservative in politics, through their conventional acceptance of the dominant group. This explains the conservatism of religious people in general, but the denominational differences are more complicated. Roman Catholics in Great Britain and the U.S.A. vote for left-wing parties even when class is held constant, probably as a result of historical traditions (pp. 82-83), perhaps also because they are a minority group. Catholics *do* have more conservative attitudes as would be expected, but this may be because conservative attitudes in these studies are defined so that official Catholic attitudes score as conservative.

It would be expected that religious conservatives would be subject to prestige suggestion. All authoritarians conform to social influence; in terms of the theory presented later this may be because they project their super-ego on to authority-figures (pp. 159-60).

The direction of causation for these variables. There is no direct evidence concerning the direction of causation. Such evidence could be obtained by studying the development of religious belief in different personalities who are equally (or not at all) exposed to the influence of different religious groups; again a study could be made of possible personality changes among people who have joined different religious bodies under social pressure. It is possible however to speculate about the direction of causation by finding out which theories best account for the facts (p. 21). The explanations given above suggest that it is the possession of certain personality traits which inclines a person towards religious beliefs and organizations. The opposite possibility was also mentioned, i.e. the social structure of a church may encourage certain personality traits.

INTELLIGENCE AND ACHIEVEMENT

Studies of children show that the more intelligent children have a more accurate knowledge of the meaning of religious concepts. On the other hand, the more intelligent children start questioning these beliefs at an earlier age (p. 62f).

A number of American studies of children and students found negative correlations between intelligence and religious beliefs, attitudes and experiences, as shown in Table 25.

TABLE 25. Religion and Intelligence

Author	Subjects	Criterion	N	Correlation of Religion and I.Q.
Howells (1928)	Psychology students	Religious conservatism	552	$-\cdot29$ to $-\cdot36$
Symington (1935)	Schoolchildren			$-\cdot13$ to $-\cdot29$ (Conservative background)
	Students			
	Research students	Religious conservatism	612	$-\cdot42$ to $-\cdot55$ (Liberal background)
Brown & Lowe (1951)	Students	Religious conservatism	788	religious S's lower (p < ·01)
Franzblau (1934)	Jewish children	Accepting traditional dogma	700	$-\cdot15$
Gilliland (1940)	Students	Attitudes to God and church	349	$-\cdot19$ to ·19 for different groups
Carlson (1934)	Students	Attitude to God	215	$-\cdot19$
Sinclair (1928)	Students	Mystical experience	500	$-\cdot27$

It can be seen that the correlation is higher for religious conservatism ($-\cdot15$ to $-\cdot55$) than for attitudes or mystical experience (·19 to $-\cdot27$). It will be noted that all these results are based on children or students, though the same result may hold for adults as well, since authoritarianism (which correlates with religious conservatism) is correlated with IQ to the extent of $-\cdot2$ to $-\cdot5$ (Christie and Jahoda, 1954, p. 168). Symington divided his subjects into those from liberal and conservative homes. It is very interesting that the correlation was higher for those from a liberal background ($-.42$ to $-.55$) than for subjects from a conservative background $(-.13$ to $-.29)$. He suggests that those from liberal homes had been freer to use their brains to discard orthodox ideas. There is little evidence about non-intellectual abilities. Sinclair (1928) and Starbuck (1926) found that students reporting mystical experiences were less good at various motor skills involving eye-hand co-ordination than other students, and that their reaction time was longer.

Other investigators have examined the proportion of religious people among the outstandingly successful. Leuba (1934) sent a questionnaire to 1,000 eminent scientists and scholars in 1914 and again in 1933. He found that 48 per cent of those classified as 'lesser' scientists believed in God, compared with 32 per cent of the 'greater' scientists. The corresponding figures for belief in immortality were 59 and 37 per cent, and the same relation held for each kind of scientist taken separately. However Fry (1933) found that 56 per cent of entries in *Who's Who* reported denominational affiliation, which is almost the same as the percentage of adults who were church members (55 per cent) at that time. On the other hand, more people claim affiliation, and even membership, than are on the church records (cf. p. 5).

Denominational differences in IQ are shown in Pratt's study (1937) of 2,080 students, the results of which are given in Table 26.

TABLE 26. Denomination and Intelligence

Episcopalians	172·8	Baptists	128·5
Christian Science	164·5	Disc. of Christ	127·8
Congregational	140·9	Methodist	127·5
Nazarene	134·5	Lutherans	126·5
Presbyterians	134·1	Miscellaneous	126·2
'Protestant'	131·0	Catholics	119·3
Evangelical	129·5	No preference	117·8

(From Pratt 1937; by permission of the Journal Press)

Fry (1933) analysed entries in *Who's Who* for 1930–1 and compared the proportion of people giving each denomination with the total membership of each denomination. The ratio of these proportions, i.e. the extent to which each denomination was over-represented in *Who's Who*, is given in Table 27.

TABLE 27. Over-representation of Denominations in *Who's Who*

Unitarian	32·5	Christian Science	1·3
Reformed	6·5	Methodist	0·9
Universalist	6·4	Baptist	0·7
Episcopalian	6·1	Disc. of Christ	0·6
Congregational	5·0	Lutheran	0·3
Quaker	4·4	Catholic	0·13
Presbyterian	3·1	Jews approx.	0·1–0·2

(From Fry 1933; by permission of the editor of *Scientific Monthly*)

It will be noticed that the main churches appear in much the same order in the two lists—one based on the intelligence of students, the other on later success. Some of the smaller bodies would not have enough representatives to be reliably sampled, at least in the student survey. It seems likely therefore that the different rates of success are due to variations in intelligence, which in turn are the product of class differences and similar factors. An additional cause may be a difference of motivation between sects. Winterbottom (1953) reports differences of child-rearing; Jews and to a lesser extent Protestants encourage independent activity in their children at an early age. This is liable to produce a greater amount of achievement motivation, which in turn enables people to become more successful.

Knapp and Goodrich (1951) show the high percentage of successful scientists coming from American liberal Arts Colleges, and the very small number from Roman Catholic universities; they suggest that Protestant ideology is more in line with scientific activity. Fry (op. cit.) also studied the professional fields in which members of each denomination became eminent. Some of these results are not surprising: for example there are no Christian Science doctors or Quaker soldiers. Others are less obvious: there are many Catholic artists, actors, and politicians, few social scientists; Unitarians produce a lot of natural scientists and social workers, but not many soldiers or politicians; Episcopalians produce a large number of soldiers, architects and engineers, but few natural scientists and agriculturists.

Super (1957) reports that not only Catholics but also Protestant groups which keep a tight control over their members, produce fewer eminent men. Kelly and Fiske (1951) found a correlation of —·39 between the strength of the religious value (Vernon-Allport) and research competence among clinical psychologists. It is possible that people taught to accept traditional ideas on authority do not so easily become innovators or research workers.

Summary. Although intelligent children grasp religious concepts earlier, they are also the first to doubt the truth of religion, and intelligent students are much less likely to accept orthodox beliefs, and rather less likely to have pro-religious attitudes or mystical experiences. There are clear differences of IQ and achievement between denominations, and the fields in which success is reached vary with denomination, scientists being largely Protestants.

Explanation. Intelligent people are less amenable to social pressure and would be expected to be unorthodox in religion as in other matters: this may be particularly true of intelligent students, who often make a point of disputing everything. Denominational differences can partly be explained in a similar way—there are fewer eminent men in religions which discourage inquiry and innovation: class differences are also partly responsible, as are denominational values in suggesting or prohibiting certain fields of activity.

DELINQUENCY AND SUICIDE

Most studies of this problem count as delinquents those people found guilty by the courts. This is an unsatisfactory definition from some points of view, for example there is known to be a bias against the working classes, since some types of middle class infringement, such as evasion of income tax, tend to be overlooked: the total number of crimes committed is unknown, the proportion discovered varying with the offence and the social class of the offender. In view of the strong link between religion and morals, it might be expected nevertheless that religious people would be better behaved and therefore get into trouble with the law less often. Using church membership or affiliation as a criterion, there is little evidence that this is so. Miner (1931) carried out an analysis comparing different states in the U.S.A. for crime rates and number of members of various denominations: he found a generally negative relationship between church membership and crime, but most of the correlations were too small to be significant. Middleton and Fay(1941) found the opposite relationship for groups of delinquent and non-delinquent girls.

It may be objected that people who are 'really religious', as opposed to being merely affiliated with a church, would not be delinquent. This could be tautological—no delinquent would be counted as being really religious. We can, however, take stricter criteria for being religious which are independent of delinquency. Glueck and Glueck (1950) compared 500 juvenile delinquents with a carefully matched control group of 500 non-delinquent children. Of the delinquent group, 39 per cent went to church weekly, compared with 67 per cent of the controls. Healy and Bronner (1923) obtained the corresponding figures of 44 per cent for the delinquents, 61 per cent for the controls. Ferguson (1952) found that 14·9 per cent of a group of 670 young people in Glasgow who were not church attenders had been convicted between the ages of 8–18, compared with 8·9 per cent for 633 regular attenders. On the other hand the mere holding of orthodox religious attitudes or beliefs does not prevent delinquency. Middleton and Fay (op. cit.) found that a group of eighty-three delinquent girls scored higher on Thurstone scales measuring attitudes towards Sunday observance and towards the Bible, though fewer of the delinquents owned Bibles. The measures used here can be regarded as tests of religious conservatism. Hightower (1930) discovered no relation whatever between Biblical information and experimental measures of honesty, suggesting that such information alone does not make for moral behaviour.

Comparing delinquency for different denominations, Trenaman found considerable differences in his study of delinquents in the British Army, as shown in Table 28.

European studies have usually found that Catholics have the highest rate, Jews and non-religious people the lowest (Lombroso, 1911; Gillin, 1945). In America, Baptists and Catholics have the highest rates (Sutherland, 1939). There is no doubt that these results can be partly explained in terms of class differences: there is a tendency for Catholics in Britain and America to be working class. On the other hand, both Catholics

TABLE 28. Delinquency and Denomination

	Delinquents	Normal Army
C. of E.	71	70
Noncon.	8	19
R.C.	20	10
Jews	1	1

(From Trenaman 1952; by permission of Methuen's and Mr. Trenaman)

and Nonconformists in Great Britain are drawn from very similar social groups (pp. 129–31), so that the higher rate for Catholics shown in Table 28 cannot be explained in this way. The low rate of crime for non-religious people in Europe may be because convicts pretend to be more religious than they really are (Miner, 1931). Some of the findings may be due to racial differences: many American Baptists are negroes (who have a high rate of crime), while American Catholics come from countries like Italy and Poland: the latter break away from their national institutions and it is the social disorganization which produces the crime (Elliott, 1952). Many English Catholics are Irish, and although the rate of crime in Ireland is

TABLE 29. The Percentages of those Sentenced for Various Crimes Belonging to Different Religious Groups

	Prot.	Cath.	Jew	No Church
Theft	52·4	43·9	1·3	1·8
Aggravated theft	58·2	37·4	1·5	2·2
Embezzlement	56·3	37·8	2·5	2·6
Swindling	53·8	38·1	4·6	2·6
Receiving stolen goods	51·5	41·1	4·9	1·9
Offences against public decency	48·7	46·9	1·9	1·7
Minor sexual offences	72·7	24·1	1·4	1·7
Rape	59·7	39·0	0·0	0·0
Sexual offences by school teachers	59·8	38·1	0·5	1·6
Rebellion against authority	52·1	43·9	1·2	2·4
Disturbance of domestic peace	58·2	38·1	0·8	2·6
Assault	56·3	40·1	1·3	2·0
Serious assault	48·2	49·3	0·6	1·5
Manslaughter and murder	58·3	38·3	0·4	2·0
Percentage of the population aged 20 and over	54·4	35·0	1·8	7·3

(From Bonger 1943)

very low, being uprooted may remove social constraints: certainly there is a very high rate of crime amongst the Irish labourers in Glasgow and Liverpool.

If delinquents are analysed by type of crime, interesting denominational differences appear. Table 29 shows the results of such an analysis of crimes in the Netherlands for the years 1910–15 and 1919. It will be noticed that Catholics have a high rate of crimes of violence, Protestants of sexual offences and Jews of fraud. It seems that there is no incompatibility between religion and crimes of all sorts; indeed Pearce (1952), reporting on his clinical experience in England, says that he has come across a number of pious blackmailers and homosexual male prostitutes.

*   *   *   *   *

Turning now to suicide, there is no evidence available on the relation with church membership or attendance. The general finding on denominational differences is that Protestants have a higher rate than Catholics. Durkheim (1897) drew attention to this fact, using statistics for different districts in Germany, collected by Morselli and von Mayr. Using these and other data, Halbwachs (1930) concludes that the suicide rate for Protestants is two to three times the rate for Catholics. American statistics are limited because religion is not entered on death certificates, but several small studies confirm Durkheim's hypothesis (Dublin, 1933). When whole nations are compared, there is a tendency for Catholic countries to have lower suicide rates than Protestant countries, but this difference is confounded with a tendency towards higher rates in economically advanced areas like the U.S.A. and Scandinavia. There is some possibility of error in these figures, since doubtful instances might not be classified as suicides in Catholic areas in view of the serious view which the Church takes of suicide. Statistics collected in Europe before 1914, and in the U.S.A. more recently, show that Jews have an even lower rate than Catholics, Since then, the rate of suicide for European Jews has risen considerably. This increase cannot be due solely to anti-semitism, since changes were observed between 1908–1923 (Dublin, op. cit., Cavan, 1928).

*   *   *   *   *

Summary. The rate of crime is lower for people who actually go to church regularly; it is no lower for people who merely hold orthodox beliefs. The rate is higher for Catholics and lower for Protestants and Jews in all countries, though this is partly due to class differences. Catholics have a particularly high rate for crimes of violence, while Protestants have a slightly above-average rate for sexual offences and Jews for fraud. Suicide is lowest for Catholics, highest for Protestants.

The direction of causation. The lower rate of crime for church attenders could be due to religious influences—though Sutherland (1939) reports that compulsory attendance for convicts produces negative results. More probably there is a statistical tendency for people of a certain personality structure to prefer religion of a certain kind, and crime of a certain kind also. The low rate of suicide for Catholics could be due to religious teaching or to the personality structure of Catholics.

Explanation. Many of these results can be explained by the theory that Catholics are 'extrapunitive' and Protestants 'intropunitive'. This explains why Catholics are more delinquent especially committing crimes of violence, and why Protestants have a higher rate of suicide: Catholics direct their aggression outwards, Protestants direct it towards themselves. Jews are low both for suicide and crime and can be regarded as 'impunitive'. The low rate of delinquency for church attenders was found in a generally Protestant context, and could be due to the stronger super-ego of serious Protestants (pp. 157–9). Alternative explanations of the low Catholic rate of suicide are the great moral pressure against it by the Church, and the possibly greater cohesiveness of Catholic communities suggested by Durkheim.

IX

RELIGION AND MENTAL DISORDER

Do religious people tend to be more or less mentally disordered on average than non-religious people? That is the main empirical question to be tackled in this section. Before reviewing the evidence on this issue, it is necessary to say something about the view that religion is *in itself* a form of disorder (or the reverse), i.e. being religious is a mark of maladjustment, just as feeling excessive anxiety or having delusions are. To deal with this suggestion it is first necessary to give some definition of 'mental disorder', in order to see if being religious could fall under it. There are people who undergo treatment either because they seek it themselves or because they are judged by others to be dangerous or incapable; all of them are generally regarded as suffering from some kind of mental disorder, and they are further classified into a number of specific syndromes. In addition there are a lot of people who have exactly the same symptoms but who escape treatment (or in mild cases do not need it); these would also be regarded as suffering from the appropriate disorders. Thus it would be quite legitimate to point to some kind of behaviour—such as having delusions—and say that non-patients who exhibit it are disordered, since this is something which is usually associated with coming for treatment. Thus, if patients were much more religious than non-patients it would be sensible to say that religion was a disorder; in other words it depends on the sheer empirical relation to be discussed below. However, some writers have supposed *a priori* that religion was a mark of insanity or the reverse in the absence of such evidence. Cameron (1947) lists 'cosmic consciousness' as a kind of psychosis, while Cavan (1949) uses the

Note. Summaries are given at the end of each section in this chapter; the direction of causation and explanation appear at the end.

amount of religious participation as part of an index of the degree of adjustment of old people. It is possible to argue in the abstract as to whether being religious or irreligious is to be better adjusted (e.g. Weatherhead, 1951, p. 412f.), but the answer will clearly depend on the beliefs of the advocate.

Even if there were no empirical relation between religion and mental disorder, it might still be sensible to give an explanation of religious behaviour by classifying it with some disorder. Freud for instance says that ritualistic religion is a kind of obsessional neurosis. He is making the perfectly legitimate suggestion that religious behaviour may be produced by similar dynamic mechanisms to those producing obsessional behaviour. The evidence for this theory is reviewed later (pp. 164–7), and is found on the whole not to support it.

We can now proceed with the *empirical* as opposed to the *logical* relations between religion and disorder. In view of what has been said it is clearly important that disorder should be defined independently of being religious: we must be on the watch, for example, that cosmic consciousness is not being used as a criterion of psychosis. If we want to know whether mystics are psychotic or not we must examine aspects of their behaviour and experience other than their mysticism.

NEUROSIS

By neurosis is meant the clinical condition known as hysteria, anxiety states and obsessional and compulsive neurosis. Neurosis is not an all-or-none affair, and estimates of its frequency in the population vary between 5–15 per cent, depending on the strictness of the criteria used. Neurosis is defined in some of the studies that follow by judgements of clinical psychologists and psychiatrists, in others by scores on mental tests which may or may not have been satisfactorily validated against such judgements.

The most extensive British study of this problem is Slater's analysis (1947) of the religious denominations of non-commissioned servicemen admitted to the Sutton Emergency Hospital in England during the last war. Out of the 13,556 admitted, 9,354 were placed in the neuro-psychiatric wards, and 4,202 in the general wards. About 77 per cent of the former were classified as neurotic. The men placed in the general ward can be regarded as representative of the Army as a whole and used as a control. The percentages of each denomination placed in the neuro-psychiatric wards are given in Table 30.

TABLE 30. The Percentages of Neuro-Psychiatric Cases of Different Denominations at the Sutton Emergency Hospital (Computed from Slater, 1947)

C. of E.	61 per cent
R.C.	72 per cent
Methodist	74 per cent
Salvation Army	85 per cent
Jews	92 per cent
Total	69 per cent

If we bear in mind that the majority of people who claim to be 'C. of E.' actually go to church very rarely, compared with members of other faiths, the Church of England members can be regarded as on average less active than the others. This suggests a slightly higher neurosis rate—at least for Army breakdowns—for religious people.

Two American studies confirm the higher rate of neurosis among Jews. Roberts and Myers (1954) carried out an analysis of all patients under treatment in New Haven, Connecticut, on December 1st, 1950: 24 per cent of the neurotic patients were Jewish, although Jews only comprised 9·5 per cent of the total population. Dayton (1940) analysed the 89,190 first admissions in Massachusetts between 1917 and 1933: 9·54 per cent of the neurotic cases were Jewish, compared with 3·91 per cent in the total population. The neurosis rate for American Jews can partly be accounted for by class differences—there are more Jews in the upper and middle classes, there is also more neurosis, perhaps because these people can afford the treatment. Again, it may be that Jews accept the idea of psychiatry more than other people, and seek treatment more often. Finally, it may be membership of a minority group rather than anything intrinsic to the religion which is responsible: it is notable that Slater found a considerable increase in Jewish neurosis between 1939 and 1945. However, in view of the very large difference in neurosis rates—Jews have approximately 2½ times the average expectancy—we shall retain this as an established result.

Several psychometric studies have been carried out in America. Funk (1956) found a correlation of ·29 between scores on the Taylor anxiety scale and a measure for orthodoxy of belief, using 255 students of Elementary Psychology aged 17–19. Dreger (1952) selected the thirty most orthodox and the thirty most liberal out of 490 members of different Californian churches. The orthodox scored higher on ego-defensiveness and dependency measured by various projection tests. Two studies of old people reached rather different conclusions. Moberg (1953) studied 219 people over the age of 65 living in institutions; a composite measure of religious activity correlated ·59 with an index of adjustment; beliefs correlated ·46 with the same index. Cavan (1949) included religious attitudes as part of a longer scale for measuring adjustment in old age, the items being selected by a panel of judges. The religious part of the scale correlated ·14–·49 with other parts of the scale, and the scale correlated well with various measures of adjustment. French (1947) reports a series of intensive clinical studies of thirty-nine subjects. She concludes that those with clearer, more differentiated beliefs—whether religious or irreligious—had a firmer ego structure with less repression and projection. This is an interesting hypothesis, but the particular study does not demonstrate it since most of the highly differentiated subjects were faculty members, while most of the others were undergraduates.

A number of investigators have given personality questionnaires to theological students and compared their scores with student norms or with actual control groups. These studies are summarized in Table 31. As can be seen from the final column, there is no consistent finding from these researches. If the first three, which are based on Catholic subjects, are compared with the rest, there appears to be a tendency for Catholic ordinands to be neurotic, while the reverse is more generally true for the Protestants. These studies all used questionnaire measures of personality, some of which are known to be of very low validity.* In particular, the Bernreuter and Bell inventories have poor validity, while little is known about some of the other tests

*See Ellis (1946) for a summary of validation studies of these tests.

Author	Subjects	N	Tests used	Control for comparison	Above or below control in adjustment
McCarthy (1942)	R.C. Seminary students	229	Bernreuter. B₁ – N (neurotic tendency) Bell. Total adjustment Flanagan. Confidence	Published norms for students	below below below
Sward (1931)	R.C. Seminary students	80	Heidbreder self-rating scales Inferiority complex	2,347 students 68 faculty 52 businessmen	below
Peters (1942)	R.C. Novices in convent	148	Bernreuter. B₁ – N	Published norms for students	same
Brown and Lowe (1951)	Prot. and Cath. students inc. Bible College members	788	MMPI. Hysteria scale Lie scale Depression and worry MMPI. (modified) emotional stability morale	The non-religious students in the sample tested	below below above above above
Johnson (1943)	Prot. Seminary students	150	Bernreuter. B₁ – N	150 salesmen	above
Cockrum (1952)	Presb. Seminary students	93	Guilford-Martin Inventory Depression Emotional stability	Published norms for students	above above
Kimber (1947)	Prot. Bible Institute students	140	California Personality Inventory Self-adjustment Social adjustment	Published norms for students	below below

used here. The most valid are probably the MMPI, the California personality Inventory and the Guilford-Martin Inventory. However, the three studies using them still give contrary findings.

There are several studies of increases in the number of mental patients suffering from 'religious excitement' or 'exaltation' at the time of revival movements. Stone (1934) carried out an interesting analysis of admissions to the New Hampshire State Hospital for three months in 1842–3, during the height of the Millerite Second Adventist movement in New England. Out of 100 admissions, twenty-four were judged to have 'religious excitement' as a result of attending Miller's meetings. Of the twenty-four, eighteen were diagnosed manic, three depressive and two catatonic. Farr and Howe (1932) give an analysis of hospital records for a number of American states for the year 1848. 'Religious excitement' is given as the diagnosis in 14·7 to 0·8 per cent of cases, the median State percentage being 7 per cent. Stone reports that at the Salpêtrière in Paris the pre-revolution percentage of patients with this diagnosis was 20–25 per cent, but this had almost disappeared by 1828. Similarly during the Welsh revival of 1905 there was an increase of the cases suffering from 'religious exaltation' from 1 to 6 per cent of cases received. At the same time the number of cases due to alcoholism fell from 16 to 12 per cent, while police records for the same fell from 10,686 to 5,673 per year in the county of Glamorgan. Nowadays patients of the same symptoms tend to be diagnosed as hysterics. It seems likely that hysterics—who can be regarded as extroverted neurotics (Eysenck, 1947)—tend to become temporarily very excited as a result of these meetings.

Summary. (a) Several of the findings discussed in this section can be summarized by saying that for people between the ages of 16–30 the religious individuals are somewhat more neurotic. This covers the findings that the neurosis rate was higher in the British Army for denominations other than the Church of England, that orthodoxy of belief is associated with anxiety and ego-defensiveness among American students, that Catholic ordinands are more neurotic than other students (though this is not the case with Protestant ordinands) and that hysterics tend to become hypomanically excited at revival meetings. (*b*) Old people who are religious are *better* adjusted than those who are not. (*c*) Jews have approximately $2\frac{1}{2}$ times the neurosis rate of Catholics and Protestants, though this might be explained in other ways.

PSYCHOSIS

By the psychoses we mean the clinical conditions of schizophrenia, mania and depression, paranoia, epilepsy, together with certain organic states, as recognized by psychiatrists. Compared with the neuroses, these conditions are rare—including less than 1 per cent of the population at any given time. Thus studies of the relation between religion and psychosis generally consist of investigations of mental hospital populations.

The first question is whether psychotic patients are more or less religious than non-patients. There are studies reporting on the religiosity of mental patients. Farr and Howe (1932) examined 500 consecutive cases, out of which sixty-eight, or $13\frac{1}{2}$ per cent, were judged to have a 'definite religious content' to their illness. These figures do not tell us whether psychotics are more or less religious than other people in the sense of going to church, holding orthodox beliefs, and the rest. What they show us is the number of patients in whom the disorder itself has a religious content, such as exhibiting delusions of a religious character. This is qualitatively different from ordinary religious experience, and probably from neurotic religion. The religious psychotics often make use of conventional religious ideas, but adapt them to their own purposes—giving themselves a more important part in the story, or modifying it in some other way.

Kaufman (1939) has developed Freud's thesis that the ideas of psychotics are simply individual religions, while ordinary religious ideas are the result of more widely shared psychological mechanisms. The same beliefs would not lead to a diagnosis of psychosis if it appeared that the patient was a member of a religious group holding these ideas (Oates, 1957). When common religious ideas are insufficient to solve a person's problems, he then constructs a weird and personal new version, for example that he himself is the Messiah.

Denominational differences have been found in the predominant types of psychosis. The most extensive study is

Dayton's (1940), referred to above. He found that Catholics had a rate for alcoholic psychosis which was 40 per cent above average, as well as a slightly higher rate for schizophrenia ($8\frac{1}{2}$ per cent above). Protestants were 39 per cent above average for senile psychosis, 34 per cent above for cerebral arteriosclerosis. Jews, as stated previously, were 144 per cent too high for neurosis and in addition were 69 per cent above average for manic depression. Roberts and Myers (1954) found a higher rate of epilepsy for Catholics, though this could be because epilepsy is commoner among the later children of large families. Some of these differences must be due to social class—the working classes have higher rates of alcoholic psychosis and schizophrenia, the upper and middle classes have higher rates for manic depression and neurosis (Rose, 1956).

We turn now to evidence about the religion of particular kinds of psychotic. It was stated above that 'religious excitement' cases are nowadays generally classified as hysteric. However, there is no hard and fast line, and we find Bender and Yarrell (1938) classifying half of a group of eighteen hospitalized followers of Father Divine as manic. Farr and Howe (1932) found that 64 per cent of the patients with religious symptoms were diagnosed manic or depressive, compared with 50 per cent for the whole 500 studied. Very few of them were suffering from religious excitement. These authors also report a previous analysis by Strecker, who found religious ideas most frequently in the affective psychoses—in twenty-eight out of 100 such cases studied.

It is commonly reported in textbooks of psychiatry that schizophrenics have religious ideas (e.g. Mayer-Gross, et al., 1954, Henderson and Gillespie, 1956). By this is presumably meant that schizophrenic patients show more 'religious' symptoms than other patients—though it was reported above that the affective psychoses show more. It seems that catatonic schizophrenics in particular are extremely preoccupied with ultimate problems, including religious ones, and have rather bizarre religious notions reminiscent of primitive myths and of the Middle Ages. They may hear voices saying things like 'Yea, we will relish thee'. Some cases think they are Christ and want to be sacrificed, while catatonics adopt religious postures such as that of Christ on the Cross (Boisen, 1955).

Paranoid patients may be religious in the sense of imagining themselves to be famous religious figures. This is also true of schizophrenics, but the latter are more chaotic and harbour a number of unrelated fantasies and identifications simultaneously. Pearson and Ferguson (1953) diagnosed twelve hospitalized nuns as being predominantly paranoid, and claim that the religious life had postponed breakdown by providing a partial adjustment.

The textbooks say that epileptics are religious too: they have 'a "religiosity" which consists largely in interlarding conversations with oily and sanctimonious religious phrases and platitudes, that are devoid of sincerity or inner feeling' (Mayer-Gross, *et al.*, 1954, p. 385); they may have delusions of being Christ, though these are less permanent than the schizophrenic's (Henderson and Gillespie, 1956, p. 133); Leuba (1925) has likened the experience of ecstatic aura in epilepsy to mystical experiences themselves. Again it is not clear that epileptics as a group are more religious in the ordinary sense. Fleck (1935) reports on 157 patients only about 20 per cent of whom were said to have a positive conformist attitude to religion.

Summary. (*a*) There is no evidence that psychotics are either more or less religious in the senses considered previously. (*b*) About one psychotic patient in seven has a definite religious content to his disorder—a bizarre personal type of religiosity. (*c*) Manic and depressive patients most often show religious symptoms; schizophrenics and paranoids have delusions and hallucinations, epileptics may have religious experiences during their fits.

MENTAL DISORDER IN RELIGIOUS LEADERS

It has been shown above that many psychotics believe themselves to be religious leaders, prophets or mystics, while many neurotics are very religious. We must now examine the evidence for the converse—are the people who become accepted as religious leaders psychologically disordered? This is a straightforward empirical question about the relation between two quite separate systems of classification; the reason it sounds startling is because there is a conflict of values—religious leaders are revered, psychotics are not. However there is at least one instance of a person who fell into both categories: Ludwig Christian Haeusser was twice diagnosed as a manic-depressive at the Hamburg University Clinic, and obtained 40,000 votes for his politico-religious party whose aim was to make Haeusser World President (Weygandt, 1926). There are a number of instances of individuals who were accepted locally as the Messiah for a short time: there were over twenty messianic movements among the North American Indians at the end of the last century (Barber, 1941), and there have been at least six English Messiahs who attracted some following (Matthews, 1936). Biographical details of the English Messiahs are provided by Matthews, who concludes that three were suffering from paranoid schizophrenia, and one each from paranoia, hysteria and mania. Other writers have attempted clinical diagnoses of more eminent religious leaders on the basis of what evidence is available. William James said 'you will in point of fact hardly find a religious leader of any kind in whose life there is no record of automatisms. . . . Saint Paul had his visions, his ecstasies, his gift of tongues, small as was the importance he attached to the latter. The whole array of Christian saints and heresiarchs, including the greatest, the Barnards, the Loyolas, the Luthers, the Foxes, the Wesleys, had their visions, rapt conditions, guiding impressions and "openings".' (1902, p. 467.) The view that many of the well-known mediaeval mystics, like St. Theresa, had marked symptoms of hysteria, has been expressed by many psychologists, as well as by writers like Evelyn Underhill (1911). Father Thurston (1951) says that most of those who have received the stigmata have been women of hysterical personality. Other well-known religious men may have been epileptic: this was certainly the case with Dostoievsky, and may have been with St. Paul—this is at any rate one explanation of his experiences on the road to Damascus (Weatherhead, 1951); Boisen gives a case-study of a Pentecostalist leader who was an epileptic (1955). William James (op. cit.) describes a number of people such as Bunyan, Tolstoy and St. Augustine who showed marked signs of melancholia, and how some of these managed to throw off their despair and preoccupation with evil by conversion.

We have now moved from those people primarily regarded as psychotic who have religious ideas, through people with psychotic symptoms who obtain some religious recognition and following, to some of the great religious leaders. The most obvious practical distinction between those in the first group and those in the last is that the latter were widely accepted as leaders whereas the others were not. The religious difference presumably is that one group were genuine, the other bogus, although it is clear that there has been some difficulty in drawing the distinction in a number of instances. What is the *psychological* difference between the two groups? There must be some empirical difference which determines the different fates of the two groups. This need not however be a difference in personality structure, it could be a sociological or historical difference—leaders are only accepted if the times are ripe, and those who were revered as mystics in the Middle Ages might be hospitalized today. It is probable that there is a personality difference as well: successful leaders of any kind have to be more in touch with other people and to be more skilful organizers than are most psychotics. Boisen (1955) suggests that the Hebrew prophets resembled acute schizophrenics, but were reacting to social problems rather than personal stress and failure, and achieved new insights valuable for others as opposed to mere idiosyncratic belief systems. Underhill (1911) suggests that the mediaeval mystics resembled hysterics except that the mystics were dominated by the idea of perceiving God rather than by some trivial and morbid notion. Another possibility is that the great leaders had psychotic episodes, during which they had vivid and sustaining religious experiences, but that they also had periods of productive activity in the world: this pattern of 'withdrawal-and-return' in creative religious personalities was pointed out by Toynbee (1946). It should be mentioned however that just as there are certain leaders, like St. Paul, whom many psychologists have regarded as disordered, so there are others, like Buddha and Christ, of whom this has not been said and who showed no obvious signs of being psychotic.

Summary. Some minor religious leaders have clearly been suffering from paranoia, hysteria, schizophrenia or other mental disorders. Many well-known religious leaders and mystics have had symptoms resembling those of the same disorders, but have also lived more organized and productive lives than would be possible had they been genuinely mad.

'EXPERIMENTAL PSYCHOSES' INDUCED BY DRUGS

It is possible to induce psychotic-like states in normal people by giving them certain drugs: such experiments are of importance since they throw light on the physiological basis of the psychoses proper. Some people have religious experiences when under the influence of the drug, and certain primitive societies make regular use of the same drugs for religious purposes.

A number of drugs produce quasi-mystical experiences, the best-known being mescaline. Weir Mitchell (1895) was the first to give a full description of these experiences, and since then many people have reported on their own experiences and those of groups of subjects to whom it has been administered. Although the results produced vary widely between subjects, and for the same subject on different occasions, several phenomena occur fairly constantly. *Hallucinations* appear when the eyes are shut; these are of a blinding brightness and are highly coloured; they are symmetrical and usually take the form of lattices, cobwebs and spirals, though human beings and flowers may also be seen. Mitchell (op. cit.) and others emphasize the indescribable splendour of these visions. *Perception* is changed in various ways: ordinary objects become more vivid, contrasts are emphasized, objects move about and are misinterpreted fantastically, while space seems greatly extended; sounds are misinterpreted in a paranoid manner, and there are delusions of persecution and grandeur. *Time perception* is similarly distorted, and subjects may have experiences of timelessness. A *mood* of ecstatic euphoria is common in which subjects feel in touch with a more basic reality—as if the veil of appearance has been rolled away; they feel as if they are just about to grasp some important truth, and have a kind of 'free-floating certainty' about things in general. *Thought processes* are however considerably impaired: there is a falling off in performance at tasks, there is flight of ideas, with blocking of deliberate thought. *Depersonalization* usually occurs, in which the personality is fragmented, as in schizophrenia, and there is a feeling of unreality about the self. (Klüver, 1928; Stockings, 1940; McKellar, 1957). Not all people have these experiences—William James for example had no experience after taking mescaline though he did with nitrous oxide. Furthermore the experiences seem to vary with the personality and beliefs of the subject, as will be shown later. Several other drugs are known to have rather similar effects, notably hasheesh, lysergic acid, and nitrous oxide; McKellar (op. cit.) has found that hypnagogic visions—experienced on the verge of sleep—are very similar.

Various religious groups have used other methods of producing religious experiences, such as fasting, flagellation, and the breathing and other exercises of Yoga. It may be that there is some physiological common denominator in all these methods.

Religious groups throughout the world have at different times made use of drugs to produce religious experiences. One of the most interesting for our purposes is the Peyote cult.* The pharmacologist Lewin discovered in 1888 that the 'buttons' of the species of cactus known as peyote in fact contained mescaline: the visions experienced by these tribes are much the same as those described above. Peyote grows in large quantities in Mexico, and it seems likely that the use of it in religious ritual goes back to Aztec times. Until 1880 the cult was confined to Mexican tribes, but when tribal warfare ceased and communications improved, it spread rapidly north to the American Indian tribes in the plains, until over forty tribes in the area were practising it. There is a lot of local variation in the rituals practised, but there are many common features. A number of pilgrims make a ceremonial trip lasting several weeks to collect the peyote buttons, during which they eat some themselves. On their return, an all-night ceremony is held: members form a circle round a crescent-shaped earthen mound and a ceremonially-built fire. At the meeting, peyote is eaten, there is singing and dancing, public confession of sins and 'doctoring' of the sick. In some Mexican tribes, the Roman Catholic influence can be seen, while in some of the American versions, like the Native American Church in Oklahoma, there is Protestant influence. The Bible is used by some groups, together with some Christian rituals and hymns.

*The best account is by La Barre, 1938.

The mescaline research has aroused considerable interest among psychiatrists, many of whom regard it as a source of 'experimental psychoses' in normal people. It is maintained that if the precise symptoms of some psychosis can be produced by a drug, then that must be the active principle producing the disorder in psychotics. Stockings (1940) argues that the effects of mescaline are very similar to those of acute schizophrenia and to toxic confusional psychosis. He points out the similarity between the mescaline condition and these psychoses in the withdrawal from reality and creation of a fantastic dream world, the feeling of living in another world, together with the hallucinations, delusions, thinking disorders and physical symptoms.

On the other hand, mescaline does produce symptoms specific to itself, such as refusal of food and sleep, and the special quality of the visual hallucinations. While schizophrenics have auditory rather than visual hallucinations, they often do have such visual experiences, and their drawings resemble the experiences of mescaline subjects. Mayer-Gross (1951) is more sceptical and suggests that the main similarity between mescaline and genuine psychosis lies in 'the strangeness experienced by the patient and the difficulty in describing what is happening.' Osmond and Smythies (1952) reply by giving a detailed list of the points of similarity between the two conditions, and pointing out that it is remarkable that they have so much in common considering the differences in the life situation of experimental subjects and mental patients. As Stockings says, subjects under mescaline produce a medley of all known psychotic symptoms at random in a short space of time, just as psychotics rarely conform to the text-book but show a rather slower variation of symptoms: this suggests a unity between the various psychoses on the one hand and the effects of these drugs on the other. However it is acute schizophrenia which most resembles 'mescaline psychosis', and Ardis has described a number of psychotic patients whose reported experiences resembled mescaline psychosis more than the classical type of psychosis (quoted McKellar, 1957, p. 111n.).

We must now discuss how far the effects of drugs resemble mystical experiences proper. There are obviously some points of similarity—the feeling of being in touch with a deeper reality, the brilliant illumination, the experience of timelessness and the loss of self. Zaehner (1957) argues that the mescaline experiences as described by Huxley (1954) is different from the experiences of the Christian mystics, who feel that they are in contact with God. Zaehner would like to maintain a supernatural explanation of Christian mysticism in contrast with a naturalistic explanation of Huxley's—a philosophical position criticized by Farrell (1955). There is some evidence, however, that a person's experiences under drugs are affected by the beliefs he already possesses. As Zaehner observes, Huxley was steeped in Eastern thought, which may explain why he had pantheistic experiences. Some subjects in mescaline experiments had 'hallucinations of supernatural figures and voices' giving rise to 'ideas of communion with God, and being divinely inspired' (Stockings op. cit., p. 35). In the Mexican Peyote tribes which have been influenced by Roman Catholicism, the members see the Virgin Mary in their visions (La Barre, op. cit., p. 162). Other differences between the two kinds of experience might be accounted for by small differences in the chemistry of the active agents. Thus it can be argued that there are two factors operative in a mystical experience—the action of a drug on the central nervous system together with a set of beliefs giving the experience a particular form.

Concerning the physiological mechanisms which produce these phenomena, there is as yet no agreed theory. Clearly the visual centre is primarily affected, but the disturbance may be one which can attack different sensory centres in turn, and which acts more on the auditory area in the case of schizophrenics. The lattice shapes seen by mescaline subjects resemble the shapes seen by patients with organic lesions in the visual cortex (McClay and Guttmann, 1941). Mescaline itself does not occur in the body naturally, but adrenalin which is chemically very similar does, and psychological stress both releases adrenalin and precipitates schizophrenia. Osmond and Smythies (op. cit.) suggest accordingly that some chemical similar to adrenalin and mescaline may be the active agent in schizophrenia. The stimulation of the thalamus and the inhibition of oxidation in the brain have also been suggested as explanations.

The question may be asked—why do these particular physiological states tend to be experienced as 'religious'? Leuba (1925) suggests that under the influence of drugs, anxiety and frustration are removed and there is a feeling of freedom and power: 'religion and the enhancement of life are inseparably associated' (p. 35). Why do other drugs like alcohol not produce religious experiences? Perhaps it is only a narrow range of physiological states which come to be defined and interpreted as religious.

Summary. Drugs like mescaline produce vivid hallucinations and other experiences somewhat resembling mystical experiences as they are reported. Some subjects do describe their drug experiences as religious, and Mexican tribes use mescaline for religious purposes—the experiences varying with the beliefs held. The effects of these drugs are also very similar to certain psychotic conditions.

The causal relations between religion and mental disorder. So far we have simply been concerned with the correlations between religion and disorder; it is now necessary to ask which way the causal influences are operating. Does the amount of religious activity influence the level of adjustment, or vice versa? Or is each determined independently by other variables? Both Farr and Howe (1932) and Oates (1949) give a classification, according to which religion is causal for some, and the disorder causal for others, of the religious psychotics concerned. About 20 per cent of these patients are said to have religious conflicts or excitement as a precipitating cause of the disorder—for example, conflicts between religion and sex. Another 35 per cent had social or moral conflicts over religion—for example, disagreements with their family over religious issues. About 45 per cent simply had religious symptoms, such as ideas of guilt, where the disorder had used religious ideas for its content, but where these were not judged to be causal. It may be noted that these authors do not mention the third possibility—that the religion and the disorder could be independently caused so that their relation is spurious. However, since the religiosity is an integral part of the disorder for psychotics, as described above, this is perhaps less likely.

The classification just described depends on inferences from the details of each case. It is very hard to see how such a diagnosis can be made on the kind of evidence available. A patient may give verbal evidence of precipitating religious conflicts—as in the case of a patient who felt suicidal during Holy Week. However, the real cause may be quite different and not conscious to the patient—for example the suicide rate increases during the spring, for reasons which are not understood by psychiatrists or conscious to their patients. Again, Hunt (1939) gives a very interesting account of fifteen boys, some of whom were initiated into homosexuality and bestiality, some into a Pentecostal church: all seven who joined both became psychotic, and case material supports the idea that conflicts between sexual desires and guilt were responsible. However, only some of the boys became homosexual, and only some became religious, in the same environment. It is possible that those with inherited psychotic tendencies tended to get themselves into conflict situations of this type. In order to demonstrate causation, material of a more experimental kind is necessary, as was argued in Chapter 3.

We can now examine the general theories which have been put forward concerning the relation of religion and mental disorders. First, there are theories in which religion is regarded as causal—religion increases or reduces disorders respectively. The theory that religion can be a cause of disorder is given little support by clinical material. As argued above, the religious conflicts observed in patients may be only apparently causal: they may instead be the ways in which patients have developed or rationalized their conflicts. Cronin (1934) decided that religious conflicts were never causal for his neurotic patients—who had simply projected deeper conflicts into this frame of reference. Turning to other kinds of data, the co-variation of cases of 'religious excitement' with religious revivals is more convincing evidence of the causal influence of religion. It is of course only a part-cause since only certain people—hysterics—become affected: their condition temporarily deteriorates. Apart from this there is really no evidence which demonstrates that religion produces mental disorder. In any case this could not be generally true, since the two are only positively associated for neurosis in young people, while there is no evidence that psychotics were unusually religious before their breakdown.

A second theory is that religion prevents mental disorders.

Jung and his followers are well known for their view that religion is necessary as an adjunct to psychotherapy. 'Among all my patients in the second half of life—that is to say, over thirty-five—there has not been one whose problem in the last resort was not that of finding a religious outlook in life. . . . It is safe to say that every one of them fell ill because he had lost that which the living religions of every age have given to their followers, and none of them has been really healed who did not regard his religious outlook' (1933, p. 264). This view is also expounded by Weatherhead (1951) who suggests specific ways in which religion can be therapeutic: (*a*) confession and acceptance of forgiveness should help with guilt feelings, 'The forgiveness of God is, in my opinion, the most powerful therapeutic idea in the world' (p. 388); (*b*) being loved by God and accepted by the church group should help those deprived of love; (*c*) the love of Christ should displace other undesirable emotional states, such as anger and fear.

This point of view can also be expressed by saying that being religious is an alternative to being neurotic or psychotic: people subjected to certain genetic or environmental circumstances will normally be (say) neurotic, unless they come under the influence of religion, in which case they will become religious instead. This appears to be Freud's view, as put forward in *Civilisation and its Discontents* (1939), where he lists religion and neurosis as part of a longer list of alternative ways of adjusting to the frustrations of civilization.

What is the empirical evidence for this point of view? To begin with it could only be generally true if there were an inverse relationship between being religious and being disordered. As we have shown, this is only the case for religion and neurosis among older people—giving some confirmation to Jung's assertion quoted above. However, it could still be the case that religious influences could be therapeutic for certain kinds of person—just as they may have the reverse effect for other kinds of people. Follow-up studies of psychotherapy with and without religious encouragement might throw light on this; no evidence is available, though there is a good deal of case-study material showing patients recovering under religious influence (e.g. Weatherhead, op. cit.). Pearson and Ferguson (1953) suggest that the peace of the convent delayed the onset of psychosis for four nuns, and Oates (1949) suggests that 20 per cent of the patients studied had 'adopted a bizarre or reactionary religion as a "last straw" attempt to cope with reality'. Although such case-studies are persuasive, they really take us no further: religious influences may be therapeutic for some patients.

The two theories discussed so far both posited religion as the causal agent. Another possibility is that the disorder is primary and the religious activity simply a result, symptom, or manifestation of this. Farr and Howe (1932) classify 45 per cent of their religious patients as having symptoms for which religion provided the content. This theory is presupposed whenever a causal mechanism for religious experience or behaviour is suggested which is of a pathological nature. For example, Flournoy (1915) describes the case of a lady who had a series of religious visions and ecstasies; he traces the pathological origins of these in the life history of the patient.

A slightly different interpretation would be that both the religion and the disorder were results of the same antecedent circumstances, though this could not very well be distinguished empirically. It might be the case that the same events produce neurosis and religion in the 16–25 age group, creating a spurious relation between the two.

To summarize this section, there is little evidence that religion ever *causes* mental disorders—apart from the states temporarily induced in hysterics by revivals—or that religion *prevents* disorders. Although young religious people have an above-average tendency to be neurotic, and psychotic patients often have religious ideas, these religious symptoms may be projections of deeper conflicts. General causal theories in this area exaggerate the extent of the relationship between religion and mental disorder, and they do not deal with the details of these relations; finally they produce no evidence concerning the direction of causation.

Explanation. The findings concerning neurosis can be explained in terms of 'dynamic' mechanisms. The neurotic instability of young religious people would be expected on the theories postulating conflict between the instincts and the super-ego as the basis of religion (pp. 156–7). The high rate of neurosis for Jews, assuming that it has not a simpler explanation, may be an important fact about Jewish character structure and be due to socialization methods: it could be connected with the religion, but none of our theories predicts this. The association between religion and stability in old people would be expected from the frustration theory (pp. 152–3)—old people become progressively more religious through anxiety about death, while those who do not find this solution become more neurotic.

The findings about psychosis can be explained at a quite different level. It is commonly assumed that while the neuroses have a considerable psychogenic element and are disturbances of the higher centres, the psychoses are primarily caused at a more organic level. The religious experiences of psychotics can be accounted for on the physiological theory, that religious experiences are partly caused by various physiological stimuli, including the effects of certain drugs similar to the substances found in the bodies of psychotics (pp. 170–3). The bizarre religious ideas of psychotics are derived from traditional religion, distorted into idiosyncratic self-referential versions under the influence of intense motivation. The ideas aid in the interpretation of the experiences as religious, the experiences support the beliefs.

X

SEX AND MARRIAGE

SEXUAL ACTIVITY

SURVEYS of sexual activity have been carried out in both countries, notably by Kinsey in the U.S. and by Chesser for English women. These are the main sources of information for this section, since these surveys were both extensive and rigorous. Kinsey and his collaborators interviewed 5,300 men (1948) and 5,940 women (1953). Although the samples were unduly weighted with middle class people and with Jews,* they included widely varying sections of the population, and great efforts were made to avoid volunteers by interviewing 100 per cent of each group contacted. The interviews show test-retest and inter-interviewer consistency, and various ingenious cross-checks were carried out. However, in an effort to induce frankness, the questions were phrased in a way that might be expected to produce exaggeration in the answers. There is of course no final check on the validity of such interview material. Chesser (1956) aided by family doctors gave questionnaires to 6,250 English women. The chief defect in the sample is that only one-third of those approached returned the questionnaires, so that the respondents may be regarded as atypical volunteers to some extent. This does not necessarily invalidate comparisons between different groups of respondents however. Chesser's method has the advantage compared with Kinsey's of greater anonymity, so that his replies may be more honest.

Each of the surveys gives separate figures for devout and non-devout subjects, as well as denominational differences. These differences will now be examined for various types of sexual activity. By 'devout', Kinsey means 'regular attendance and/or active participation in church activities'. This criterion

*However, total scores are based on appropriately weighted means of the subgroups (1948, p. 108f.).

apparently included about 25 per cent of Protestants, 80 per cent of Catholics and 10 per cent of Jews. The index of sexual activity is either orgasms per week—the medians for each group being compared—or alternatively the percentage of each group who report the activity in question at all. Chesser uses two indices of religious activity—'regular' church attendance, and a composite index of religious upbringing.

Total sexual outlet—in terms of median orgasms per week—was lower for the devout in all the groups studied by Kinsey, male and female, married and single. The median frequency for the devout was about two-thirds that of the others, the percentage of devout people experiencing orgasm was less, and the age of onset later. Comparing denominations, Jews were least active, followed by Catholics and Protestants, not only for total output but for most kinds of sexual activity.

Pre-marital intercourse was reported by about half as many religious as other subjects in both surveys. However, this difference is less than that due to social class—pre-marital intercourse being about seven times as common for Kinsey's working class respondents as for his college graduates. Kinsey found small denominational differences—Orthodox Jews being least active, Chesser found English Jews and Nonconformists rather less active than Catholics and members of the Church of England.

Marital intercourse showed a somewhat lower frequency (three-quarters) for Kinsey's devout males. His devout females showed no difference either in frequency of intercourse or in successful orgasms—with the exception of Catholics during the first year of marriage who were less active and less successful. Terman (1948) found no relation between the religious upbringing of women and their orgasm adequacy, but this was less when their husbands had a religious background. Chesser's women who attended church regularly, reported more successful orgasms and great sexual satisfaction—but the differences were small and were not found for women who had a religious upbringing.

Masturbation was less for the devout in Kinsey's surveys, for both sexes, and for married as well as single. *Homosexuality* was slightly less for the devout; the rate was particularly low for Jews and high for Catholics, particularly non-practising Catholics.

'Petting to climax' was as common among Kinsey's devout men as for the non-religious. A smaller proportion of Kinsey's devout female sample reported this, but Chesser's devout women reported as much 'petting' as the others. This difference may be due to Kinsey's criterion of 'climax' which was not used by Chesser. Again the class differences are far greater than any differences due to religion. Chesser's Jewish women reported this more than those of other denominations. *Nocturnal emissions* for Kinsey's devout males were insignificantly more frequent, for his devout females sex dreams to the point of orgasm were less frequent.

The chief criticism that can be made of these results is that they may reflect a greater unwillingness on the part of religious people to admit to sexual activities, especially those condemned by the church. However, Kinsey took great pains to exact a full report, and Chesser's subjects were anonymous. Furthermore, the surveys largely agree with each other, and the same results are found from comparisons of sub-groups of very varied kinds.

MARITAL STATUS

A number of surveys which provide separate statistics for the married and the single indicate a much lower level of church attendance on the part of married people. Chesser (1956) found that 30 per cent of single female respondents were 'regular' church-goers compared with 16 per cent of the married. Considering that married people are older than single people on average this is even more striking, since older people (after 30) are more religious. Fichter (1952), reporting a survey of American Catholics, found single people more active on several criteria—though each involved church attendance of some kind. There is a very obvious explanation for this result—that married people are kept at home by small children.* Is there still a difference if we consider other criteria of religious activity?

Gorer (1955) gives figures on a number of separate indices as shown in Table 32.

*However Lenski (1953) found that couples with children were more likely to express 'much interest' in religion.

TABLE 32. Religious Activity and Marital Status (Gorer, 1955)

	Denom. affil.	Weekly attend.	Daily prayers	Believe in after-life	Believe in devil	Spiritualists
Single	75	21	44	48	21	2
Married	76	12	41	46	19	3
Widowed	76	26	71	62	24	10
Divorced or separated	65	12	49	44	20	7

(By permission of Cresset Press)

While single people go to church much more often than married, they are only slightly more active in prayer and belief. It seems that single people are consistently more religious than married, but that the difference is only marked for church attendance—though correction for age would probably increase the differences.

Widowed people show a rather higher rate of activity than single or married, particularly on saying daily prayers and believing in the after life. They are older on average and this may account for the difference. However, the widowed also tend to believe in spiritualism and to believe that they will rejoin loved ones in the after-life (Gorer, op. cit., p. 258).

Divorced and separated people will be older on average than married people, probably not much younger than the widowed. On an age basis alone we would expect them to be intermediate between married and widowed. In fact, they are similar to married people except that they pray more often and belong to a church less frequently. They also have the same low rate of church attendance as married people, without the explanation of small children keeping them away. The explanation may be that some churches condemn or discourage divorce so that divorced people only engage in private religious practices. Karlsson (1951) found that recently separated women in Sweden were more religious than married women; other studies show that happily married people are more religious, so that Karlsson's result is probably due to the need of separated people for religious consolation.

MARITAL ADJUSTMENT

Several investigators have examined the factors associated with marital happiness or 'adjustment'—this being measured by means of self-ratings. In all of the studies in which religious variables have been included, the more religious people have claimed to be more happily married. The differences are not large, but they are highly consistent. Chesser (1956) found that 91 per cent of his English married women who were regular church attenders were 'exceptionally or very happy' as compared with 62 per cent of non-attenders. Landis and Landis (1953) in a study of 409 American couples found that 54 per cent of regular attenders were 'very happy' as opposed to 43 per cent of those who went occasionally or never. Burgess and Cottrell (1939) found a 'good' marital adjustment in 50 per cent of couples married in church compared with about 37 per cent of those married elsewhere. When couples from a religious background are compared with others, the result is not so definite: Chesser found that such marriages were happy slightly more frequently—79 per cent compared with 67 per cent, and Terman (1938) found a curvilinear relationship so that those with a strict religious training or with no religious training were less happily married than those with an intermediate amount.

Locke (1951) found that 'very happy' marriages were much less common when there was agreement about religion—65 per cent compared with 9 per cent of his 544 couples in the early years of marriages. Fisher (1948) in a study of the parents of college students found evidence that similarity of religious values was more important for the success of marriage than similarity of other values on the Vernon–Allport scale. Burchinal (1957) has pointed out on the other hand that agreement on such matters as finance and how to spend time together emerge as more important predictors of marital adjustment than agreement on religion. In other studies (e.g. Landis, 1949) in which American children were asked about their parents, the divorce rate was highest for mixed Protestant-Catholic marriages, and conflict over the religious training of the children seemed to be the main source of trouble in these families. Monahan and Kephart (1954) in a careful study of desertion and non-support cases in Philadelphia did not find any more desertions in mixed marriages; Mowrer (1927) analysed 2,661 marriages in Chicago and found that mixed religion was only a factor in desertion for partners of the same race—differences of nationality outweighing differences of religion. The total number of broken families, counting both divorces and separation, is hard to estimate, but Mowrer found that the duration of marriage was less for mixed marriages.

There is some evidence concerning denominational differences in marital adjustment. Monahan and Kephart (loc. cit.) found, as would be expected, that Catholics had a lower rate of divorce than Protestants or Jews—they had 25·5 per cent of the divorces, whereas Catholics made up 40 per cent of the population. On the other hand, Catholics had a higher rate of desertion. The total number of broken families is hard to estimate, but Bell's findings (1938) suggest that Jewish families had the lowest rate of disruption, Catholic families slightly lower than Protestant.

SEXUAL ATTITUDES

Religious people of various denominations are found to have characteristic attitudes on subjects such as divorce and birth control.

Chesser (1956) found that only 5 per cent of Catholics would seek divorce if their marriage proved unsatisfactory, compared with 32 per cent of members of the Church of England. Similarly, only 14 per cent of those from a religious background said they would seek divorce, compared with 37 per cent of those from a non-religious background. In his factor analysis of the opinions of 700 people, Eysenck (1944) found that there was a high negative correlation between being in favour of easier divorce laws and agreeing with various religious propositions.

On the subject of birth control, Chesser (op. cit.) found interesting differences between denominations, as shown in Table 33.

Carlson (1934) in a factorial study in America found that

TABLE 33. Denominations and Practice of Birth Control

	C. of E.	Noncon.	R.C.	Jew	Other	None
Married	69	79	47*	82	83	75
Single (would use in a future marriage)	84	77	39			

(From Chesser 1956)

* "husband only" 28%

favourable attitudes to God and to birth control were diametrically opposed. Freedman and Whelpton (1950) however found that religious interest affected the use of contraception only in the case of the extreme religious interest groups.

Gorer (1955) found that a lower proportion of people who went to church and said prayers thought that people should have sexual experience before marriage, as shown in Table 34.

TABLE 34. Religion and Approval of Pre-Marital Intercourse

Attend Church	Approve %	Say Prayers	Approve %
More than once a week	17	More than once a day	22
Weekly	24	Daily	25
More than once a month	24	Very seldom	36
Never	40	Never	46

(From Gorer 1955; by permission of the Cresset Press)

Similarly, Eysenck (op. cit.) found approval for trial marriage opposed to agreement with religious statements.

Summary for Chapter 10. (*a*) Religious people report a lower total level of sexual activity, particularly for pre-marital intercourse, homosexuality and masturbation, to some extent for marital intercourse but not for 'petting'. These differences are greatest for Jews, followed by Catholics and Protestants.

(*b*) Widowed people have the highest level of religious activity, though this may be due to age differences. Single people are slightly more religious than married. Divorced people engage in private rather than public religion.

(*c*) Religious people report a greater degree of marital happiness. Mixed marriages break up more frequently than others. Catholics have a lower divorce rate but a higher rate of desertion.

(*d*) Religious people are opposed to divorce, birth control and pre-marital intercourse. Catholics are particularly opposed to the first two.

The Direction of Causation. An obvious interpretation of many of these findings is that they are due to the church's teachings. This is confirmed in the case of sexual behaviour by the lower rate of forbidden forms of it. On the other hand, the lower total outlet and the lower rate of marital intercourse suggest another alternative—that people who inhibit their own sexual drives also become religious. Similarly, it is likely that single people are consequently religious rather than vice versa.

Explanation. Two theories can be suggested to account for these facts. The theory that religion is a product of conflict between the super-ego and the instincts predicts a lower level of sexual activity, and opposition to sexual licence, on the part of religious people (pp. 155–7). The theory that religion is a response to frustration predicts more religious activity for the single and widowed, though the drives are different (pp. 150–2).

XI

SOCIOLOGICAL FACTORS

SOCIAL CLASS

SOCIAL class is an interesting but rather confusing variable. The social class of a person may be defined as the level in the social hierarchy at which he is accepted by others and at which he participates in the informal social life without embarrassment on either side. It is possible to find out by actual observation and extensive interviewing whereabouts people come in the hierarchy, and this has been done in several American towns by Warner and Lunt (1941). They found it possible to predict a person's social class by a suitable weighting of such variables as income, education, type of occupation and size of house. In some social surveys, interviewers rate respondents on a scale; in the Gallup polls they use a four-point scale 'Av+', 'Av', 'Av—' and 'Very Poor'. These ratings are based on the kind of factors mentioned above, taken together. In other surveys, the occupation alone is taken—again use is made of some set of categories of occupations arranged in order of social prestige. While this may be misleading for individuals, it probably serves when a large sample is being considered. The term 'social class' is sometimes used in the quite different sense of the level in the hierarchy to which the person *thinks* he belongs—which may be quite different from where others think he belongs. This is of some psychological interest but cannot be used as a predictor of religious attitudes, and in any case has very rarely been used in these surveys.

Class differences in religious activity in Great Britain are shown in Table 35, where the results of surveys by the British Institute of Public Opinion (1950) and Odham's Press (1947) are given.

Note. Summaries are given at the end of each section in this chapter.

TABLE 35. Religion and Social Class in Great Britain

	Weekly Attendance %	Favourable Attitude %
Upper and Upper Middle	19·4	20·9
Lower Middle	16·3	18·0
Working	13·4	21·9

(From Odham's Press 1947; by permission of Dr. Max Adler)

	Claim Affiliation %	Prays Regularly %
Av+	94	58
Av	90	53
Av−	91	45
Very poor	91	46

(From B.I.P.O. 1950; by permission of Dr. Henry Durant)

It can be seen that there is a tendency for the working classes to be less active on most criteria, particularly in frequency of church attendance. The only exception to this is the Odham's Press finding that they were if anything more favourable in attitude to the churches—as shown by answers to the question 'How well are the churches doing their job?' In Gorer's survey* (1955) there was a tendency for people earning less than £5 per week to be more religious, but this was probably because many of these would be old people, who are highly religious (pp. 67–69). In 1900 there was a strong tendency for the upper and middle classes to be more active in religion, as reported by observers such as Booth (1902). Without comparable statistical evidence it is not possible to say whether the 'estrangement of the working classes' has increased or not. It is certainly true that there is less religious life in large centres of industrial population, as was found by Gorer (pp. 134–6); Wickham (1957) found a steeper decline in church membership in Sheffield than for the country as a whole.

Turning now to class differences between denominations, Table 36 shows that there is a small tendency for the middle and upper classes to belong to the Church of England, rather than to the Catholic or Nonconformist churches. It is probable that this difference is less than it was in 1900, though again the necessary data do not exist. Of the small sects, Wilson (1955) found that the Elim Foursquare Gospel movement and the

*In any case Gorer's sample was not satisfactory, since his respondents as well as being volunteers were all readers of *The People*, a paper of largely working-class circulation. While his results on certain other variables are probably fairly satisfactory, those on social class are less likely to be so.

TABLE 36. Denomination and Social Class in Great Britain

G.B. 1950 *(B.I.P.O.) Private Communication*

	C. of E.	R.C.	Noncon.	C. of Scot.
Av+	55	9	13	9
Av	53	10	12	8
Av−	51	12	15	8
Very poor	48	14	17	6
Total	51	11	15	8

(Percentage of each social class who claim allegiance to the churches named)

(By permission of Dr. Henry Durant)

TABLE 37. Religion and Social Class in the U.S.A.

	Claim affiliation %	Weekly attendance %
Business and professional	83	48
White collar	82	50
Manual workers	77	44

(Gallup Poll, from Rosten 1955; by permission of Dr. Gallup and Simon & Schuster Inc.)

Christadelphians were drawn from the very poor, though this was not true of the Christian Scientists. Gorer (1955) also found more Spiritualists and other sect members amongst the very poor.

American class differences in religious activity are given in Table 37. The finding that middle class people are more concerned with religion was confirmed by Lenski (1953) who found that middle class families in Indianapolis expressed greater interest in religion than those above or below them.

Class differences between denominations are shown in Table 38, which gives the results of an analysis of four surveys carried out by the Office of Public Opinion Research during 1945–6, with a total of 12,000 respondents.

In the first place, there is a tendency for Jews to be on average of higher social class than Protestants, and Protestants than Catholics, although the class spectrum of Protestant bodies covers the whole range. Pre-war surveys did not show such a marked Protestant-Catholic difference, and it appears that there must have been a considerable change between 1939–45 (Pope, 1948). The more striking result however is the stratifica-

131

tion of the Protestant churches: there seems no doubt that the Presbyterians, Congregationalists and Episcopalians tend to come at the upper end of the scale, while the Baptists, Lutherans and small sects come at the lower end. Other surveys of particular localities have found sects such as the Pentecostalists and

TABLE 38. Denomination and Social Class in the U.S.A.

	Profes-sional	Busi-ness	White Collar	Service	Skilled and semi-skilled	Un-skilled	Farm
Presbyterian	19·7	11·2	20·7	7·9	20·2	3·3	17·0
Congregational	19·6	13·3	19·3	5·8	21·0	1·4	19·6
Episcopal	17·1	14·5	25·2	10·2	23·3	2·3	7·4
Jewish	14·4	21·7	36·5	4·3	22·3	0·2	0·6
Christian Scientist	13·4	9·7	35·1	8·9	18·7	1·5	12·7
No preference	11·7	8·2	23·3	10·5	28·3	7·1	11·0
Methodist	10·8	7·8	19·6	11·0	23·0	5·1	22·7
Disciples of Christ	9·9	6·3	14·0	9·5	25·5	5·5	29·3
'Protestant'	9·3	7·5	19·8	11·4	33·3	6·8	11·9
'Don't know'	9·2	6·6	16·4	7·9	31·1	9·5	19·3
Small Prot. sects	9·0	6·5	15·3	12·9	27·8	9·6	18·9
Mormons	9·0	5·4	15·0	6·5	15·6	19·8	28·7
Roman Catholic	7·1	6·6	23·0	13·6	35·3	5·8	8·6
Reformed	7·1	11·0	23·6	8·7	26·8	3·1	19·7
Lutheran	6·1	7·4	17·8	11·6	26·9	4·0	26·2
Baptist	6·1	5·7	14·5	15·5	29·2	6·7	22·3
National sample	10·5	8·5	20·4	11·2	27·2	5·5	16·7

(From *Information Service* 1948; by permission of Dr. Benson Y. Landis)

other 'Holy Rollers' rather lower than the results of these surveys suggest. Goldschmidt (1948) found that 84 per cent of the Pentecostalists in part of California were unskilled labourers, compared with 19 per cent for the Assembly of God, 15 per cent for the Baptists and 1 per cent for the Congregationalists. Field studies by Pope (1942) and Boisen (1955) of particular small sects have shown that these movements start among the very poor. As described above (p. 34) sects may develop into middle class denominations as the members become more prosperous. This presumably explains why small sects do not appear at the very bottom of Table 38.

Summary. In Great Britain the upper and middle classes are most active in religion, as has been the case since 1900. These groups have a slight tendency to belong to the Church of England rather than to the Nonconformist or Roman Catholic churches. In the U.S.A. the middle classes are slightly more active than those above or below: the churches with liberal tendencies such as the Congregationalist, Unitarian and Jewish come high in the social scale, and the Catholic and Fundamentalist bodies at the lower end.

Direction of Causation. It is most likely that social class influences religion rather than vice versa, although the low position of Roman Catholics may be due to the low achievement motivation of Catholics (pp. 95–96), and it is possible that the thrift encouraged by Protestantism results in social mobility, as suggested by Max Weber (1904–5). Support for the view that class position is causal, is provided by the fact that whole churches change their religious outlook after most of the members have changed their status (Boisen, 1955).

Explanation. It is shown later that the religion of small sects among the working class can be explained in terms of socioeconomic frustration (pp. 147–50). However, some of the main Protestant bodies have considerably more support from the upper and middle classes, particularly, it was suggested, churches of 'liberal' outlook in theology. Niebuhr (1929) maintains that all churches reflect the interests of the social class of the majority of their members, and Weber (op. cit.) showed the resemblance between the ideas of the Protestant Reformers and the capitalist ideology. Following this approach, Yinger (1957) argues that the American liberal Protestant churches reflect the political conservatism, nationalism, optimism and acceptance of the *status quo* of the upper middle class.

MINORITY GROUPS

Related to class differences are differences of race or caste, save that here the barrier is almost impossible to cross. The best evidence on this problem from our field of inquiry concerns the American negro. In 1946 about 71 per cent of negroes were church members compared with 55 per cent of whites (Sweet, 1948), most of them being Baptists and Methodists. Small sects also flourish among the negroes, but in all their Protestant churches there is more spontaneous and emotional behaviour than in the corresponding white denominations. The negroes were converted in the periods of white evangelism and have retained the form of worship of those times (Myrdal, 1944). It is generally agreed by sociologists that the church means more to negroes than to whites, partly because it acts as a kind of community centre. As with the Protestant churches, the poorer the neighbourhood the more other-worldly the religion, and there is usually no attempt to link religion with social reform. Yinger (1957) reviews the religious movements found among various minority groups and suggests that they can be classified into three types:—(a) those that 'passively accept their dis-privileged status, emphasising only the importance of religious values'—the small sects discussed above would fall into this category; (b) those which criticize without attacking the social order, and withdraw from society, and (c) those that protest aggressively on religious grounds against society at large. Yinger maintains, though without detailed empirical evidence, that minority group religions are more actively aggressive rather than passive, the more hopeful and powerful they are and the more the personality structures of both members and leaders are inclined towards this form of response.

Summary, etc. Minority groups tend to have an above-average level of religious activity, and to adopt forms of religion which are either completely other-worldly or aggressively critical of society. Presumably the minority group status is the causal agent here, and the explanation is similar to that of working class sect religion—it is an adaptation to frustration (p. 149).

URBAN-RURAL DIFFERENCES

Differences of religious behaviour between town and country have been found in a number of surveys, in which that parti-cular breakdown was included. Gorer (1955) found about 25 per cent more activity in the country for Great Britain as shown in Table 39; Ogburn and Tibbitts (1938) and Lenski (1952) found clear evidence of more church attendance in American country districts and small towns. Denominational differences are small in Great Britain (Gorer, op. cit.); in the U.S.A., it is found that Catholics and Jews are congregated in the large cities, while most of the Protestant denominations are over-represented in small towns and country districts (Table 39).

Explanation. Sociologically, there are important differences between communities of different sizes. Social isolation is probably greatest in the central sectors of big cities and in thinly populated parts of the country. Social integration, and its attendant pressures towards conformity, is probably greatest in small towns. Therefore, if social isolation is a factor in religion, there should be a curvilinear relation with community size, while if social pressures are a major factor there should be a curvilinear relation in the opposite direction—small towns coming out the most active. In fact, all relations with size of community turn out to be linear: this means that either the two factors mentioned are unimportant, or they balance one another out. In view of the fact that each denomination shows a distinct, yet linear, pattern it seems most probable that neither factor is of much significance—since it would be expected that some particular denomination would be more heavily dependent on one of these mechanisms than others, and produce a curvilinear result.

Another hypothesis might be that these differences are due to historical processes of various kinds. The greater activity in British country areas and small towns could be due to cultural lag—large towns taking the lead in a decline of religion as in other matters. The American results can be similarly explained: the Catholics and Jews arrived in the later phases of immigration and consequently moved into the cities, whereas the older-established Protestants had moved out into the country.

Direction of Causation. It will be noticed that the sociological explanations assume that urban/rural differences are causal, while the historical account assumes to some extent the reverse; however the evidence available does not enable us to decide on this issue.

TABLE 39. Religious Activity and Size of Community
U.S.A. 1946 (Computed from Information Service 1948)

	Farms	Under 2,500	2,500– 10,000	10,000– 100,000	100,000– 500,000	Over 500,000
Total population	16·4	8·9	20·4	20·8	13·5	20·0
Roman Catholics	·54	·68	·68	1·19	1·36	1·42
Jews	·04	0	·21	·43	·70	3·83
Methodists	1·39	1·44	1·20	·91	·78	·52
Baptists	1·33	1·18	1·11	·92	1·10	·54
Disciples of Christ	1·68	1·58	1·31	·84	·84	·13
Small sects	1·14	·95	1·24	1·00	·90	·73

(These figures are ratios actual/expected number of members; by permission of
Dr. Benson Y. Landis)

GREAT BRITAIN (Gorer 1955)

	Under 10,000	10,000– 100,000	100,000– 1,000,000	over 1,000,000
No religion	19	21	23	29
Weekly attendance	17	15	15	12
Daily prayers	48	43	42	40

(By permission of the Cresset Press)

SOCIAL DISORGANIZATION

People are said to be socially disorganized if there are no strong links of friendship, or persistent patterns of social interaction between them. The term can be applied to individuals who live alone and do not belong to or are not accepted by social groups or organizations; it can be applied to social groups where the members do not like one another—the reverse of 'cohesiveness' (Argyle, 1957, p. 123f.); it can be applied to areas or organizations where there is little formation of social groups or friendships. Hare (1952) has reviewed the evidence showing how the level of mental disorder increases with social disorganization—including people who are unmarried, immigrants, people in areas of low population density and dwellers in the disorganized central sectors of large cities. In this section we shall see if social disorganization affects religion.

Marital status has been examined in an earlier section, and it was found that the single and the widowed were slightly more religious than married people: this difference is greater for the widowed, who have been suddenly plunged into a state of social disorganization.

Urban-rural differences have been discussed in a previous section, and provide no evidence that social disorganization has any influence on religion.

There are several more direct studies of social disorganization. Gadourek (1956) found in his survey of a Dutch community that religious people actually participate in more social clubs than non-religious people. On the other hand Holt (1940) maintains that Holiness sects in America grew particularly in the new industrial areas among people who had been uprooted from other parts. Cohn (1957) in his study of millennial movements in mediaeval Europe found that these generally began under conditions of social disorganization resulting from rapid social change. However, the findings on community size (Table 39) offer no support for the theory that sects flourish amid social disorganization. In the American Army surveys on the use of prayer in battle, it was found that new troops prayed more than others (Stouffer, *et al.*, 1949); it is argued that this is because they had less group support, but it could also have been because they were fresh to battle, and were more anxious.

Summary, etc. There is little real evidence that religious activity varies with the degree of social disorganization.

ECONOMIC PROSPERITY

It has sometimes been thought that religion prospers in times of economic depression. An attempt has been made to test this hypothesis by plotting curves of *per capita* personal income (at constant prices) against the membership statistics for various churches. These curves are not reproduced here because they show virtually no relationship between the two variables. In Great Britain there has been a general increase in prosperity since 1925, accompanied by a fall in religious activity, while in America prosperity has been accompanied by a rise in the level of religion; in neither country is there any detailed correspondence between the fluctuations in the curves, as would be expected if there was any causal connexion, and is found for example between indices of economic prosperity and suicide rates (Henry and Short, 1954).

The greatest change in the level of economic prosperity since 1900 took place during the depression years of 1929–33 in Great Britain and 1930–35 in the U.S.A. The depression was welcomed by some religious leaders who thought that people would turn to the churches. In Great Britain there was a slight rise in the membership figures of the Church of England and the Roman Catholic Church, but not for the Nonconformist bodies (Fig. 1, p. 6). The American changes have been analysed in detail by Kincheloe (1937), and his main results will be reported here. During the depression there was no change of membership in the major bodies. However, there was a 10 per cent rise in voluntary contributions from 1929–32, followed by a drop to 25 per cent below the initial figure in 1935—but the rise was probably due to an active drive for funds by the churches at that time. A survey of 678 Congregational churches showed a small temporary rise of attendance (loc. cit.), but a survey of rural churches showed a decline of attendance during this period (Brunner and Lorge, 1937). Attendance of Jews at the Synagogue however dropped about 30 per cent. It seems that the influence of the depression on the main religious bodies was to produce a small initial increase of activity in some but not others: the overall effect was slight. Several writers have reported that the small Protestant sects in America expanded during the depression (e.g. Boisen, 1955). The best available figures for testing this hypothesis are to be found in the *Census of Religious Bodies*: Table 40 shows the membership returns to the *Census* between 1906–36 for a number of sects which did increase during the depression. It can be seen that they were increasing at much the same rate both before and after the depression. This is consistent with Kincheloe's estimate that sect members increased from 150,000 in 1920 to 400,000 in 1930 and 550,000 in 1935.

There is no good evidence about the British sects, which do not seem to have increased in membership since 1900. Wilson (1955) does report however that the evangelistic campaigns of the Elim Foursquare Gospel movement were most successful during the depression years.

The other large change in economic conditions has been the post-war boom, particularly in the U.S.A. This has been accom-

TABLE 40. American Sects and the Depression

	1906	1916	1926	1936	1953
Assemblies of God (thousands)	—	6·7	47·9	148	370
Church of God (thousands)	—	7·8	23·2	44·8	66·3
Church of the Nazarene (thousands)	6·7	32·3	64	136	250
Evangelical Pillar of Fire	230	1,129	2,442	4,044	5,100
Seventh Day Adventists (thousands)	62·2	79·3	111	133	261
The Pentecostal Holiness Church (thousands)	—	5·6	8·1	12·9	43·9
Pilgrim Holiness Church (thousands)	2·7	5·3	15·0	20·1	30·9

(From *Census of Religious Bodies* 1906–36 and *Yearbook of American Churches* 1955)

panied by a spectacular increase of religious activity for all churches, including the sects; in Great Britain there has been an increase in religion since 1950.

Summary. There is very little relation between religion and economic prosperity and if anything there is more religious activity during times of prosperity. While it is true that the American sects flourished during the depression, their rate of increase was much the same before and after.

Direction of Causation. Economists and psychologists generally assume that economic variables are causal: until positive evidence has been accumulated to show that people's attitudes and beliefs can affect economic conditions, this assumption must be accepted.

Explanation. It is argued elsewhere (pp. 147–50) that economic and social status deprivation is an important factor in small sect religion; it would be expected from this that the sects *would* have expanded during the depression. Henry and Short (1954) account for the similar failure of the working class suicide rate to increase by suggesting that 'relative status' is in fact raised for this group by the decline of middle-class prosperity. This suggests that it may be deprivation of status rather than money which is the more important in producing sects.

XII

THEORIES OF RELIGIOUS
BEHAVIOUR AND BELIEF

INTRODUCTION

IN the early days of psychology before about 1920, much of
the writing was of a purely descriptive variety, using anecdotal and similar evidence. Although various theories were
put forward, no attempt was made to verify them against
empirical data. In most fields of psychology the picture has
changed: detailed experimental and statistical research is conducted to discover the exact relations between empirical variables, and theories are tested by confirmation of deductions
drawn from them. In the field of the psychology of religion, the
position is rather confused: there is a lot of detailed empirical
material, and that has been reviewed in this book; on the
other hand very little use has been made of this data for testing
theories of religious behaviour, and most books on the psychology of religion make no reference to it at all. There are a
number of theories of religious behaviour, but as yet there has
been almost no attempt to see whether the empirical evidence
supports them or not. There have been isolated attempts by
writers such as Starbuck, Leuba and Thouless to test specific
hypotheses, but it is more common to find religious behaviour
explained in terms of McDougall's instincts, supported by vague
resemblances between religious and sexual behaviour, and so
forth.

In the earlier part of this book the empirical evidence has
been collected together; in this chapter a number of theories
will be stated and tested against the data. Some of these theories
were put forward imprecisely and long ago, without regard for
statistical verification. Some were put forward as clinical-
historical interpretations, with no thought of what might be

deduced from them. Most of them were intended to be explanations of the facts that people hold religious beliefs and go to church, rather than as explanations of individual differences in these activities. It is generally supposed that scientific theories* have three main functions—co-ordinating previous findings, suggesting new ones, and satisfying curiosity. A theory is taken to be confirmed if many of the empirical predictions made from it are verified. In this case the empirical findings have been stated already, so we shall see how well these can be explained by the theories.

The essential feature of a scientific theory is that empirical generalizations—both those known and those as yet undiscovered—can be deduced from it, and so explained. There are several different kinds of theory in psychology. One kind, which scarcely qualifies but is often regarded as a kind of theory, is where a number of empirical results are all subsumed under a higher-level generalization. Different results can be unified in this way by the use of somewhat abstract terms in the explanatory generalization, which can be interpreted in several ways. One example of this is the theory, discussed below, that religion is a response to frustration. The concept of frustration can be defined so that the frustration of any of a number of drives can be included. A second type of theory involves the setting up of some mechanism or model. The model can be a mechanical model, or be indicated by means of postulates. The theory that God is a projection of the super-ego is a theory of this kind: the super-ego and the instincts are pictured as conflicting entities, and the conflict can be reduced by the subject 'externalizing' one of them. The difficulty with this and other theories derived from psychoanalysis is that it is difficult to derive unambiguous predictions from them. A third kind of theory explains an empirical result by showing that it is an example of a law in another field of research—this will be called a 'same-level theory' (cf. Argyle, loc. cit.). An example of this is the classification of changes under psychotherapy as a case of 'learning'. One could verify such a claim by showing that the empirical laws governing one phenomenon are the same as those governing the other—for example showing that psychotherapy is more successful when short, frequent sessions are used, applying the

*A fuller account of theory in psychology is given in Argyle (1957), Chap. 3.

principle of the superiority of 'spaced training' which is widely true of learning. The important point is that the theory is verified by proof that the new phenomenon follows the same empirical laws as the other, and not merely by a general descriptive resemblance.

The method of verifying these theories is much the same in each case, though the details differ. The theory is stated as precisely as possible, and deductions are made about what would be expected in terms of individual differences in religious behaviour, and of the type of beliefs which would be present. For example, if religion is due to frustration, then people who are deprived of the gratification of needs should be more religious, while their beliefs should form some kind of compensation for their frustrations. This theory could be put forward as the sole explanation of religion—in which case there should be an exact correspondence between the degree of frustration and the amount of religious behaviour, or it could be put forward as one process amongst others—in which case a significant correlation of undetermined size would be expected between frustration and religion. In the case of all the theories considered in this chapter it is the second interpretation which will be given, whatever may have been the intention of earlier writers. We should perhaps go still further and make clear our belief that religion is a highly complex phenomenon for which no single theory will be adequate. There are probably aspects of religion, perhaps reflected in the data previously considered, which are not accounted for by any of the theories discussed here. However these theories are the simplest, the most often discussed, and, we shall show, the most powerful for accounting for the facts.

There are several difficulties which arise in the course of these verifications. (1) The same empirical result sometimes follows from more than one theory. There are two main possibilities here: either two separate processes are operating together, or one theory includes the other by making a wider range of successful predictions. If one theory can account for all the phenomena which the other explains, together with further results, then the narrower theory can be discarded. However, if the result which is jointly explained is one of the few points of overlap, it is more likely that two separate processes are at work, and both theories should be retained. The result in question is in this case 'overdetermined'. (2) Some of the verifications may be successful and others not. We shall deal with this by showing the areas over which the theory applies. For example, the theory may fit perfectly for certain religious groups, or for people of a certain age-range, but not for others. Furthermore, the theory may have to be made more specific in terms of the particular drives which are being frustrated, coming into conflict, and so forth. (3) The direction of causation may be specified in the prediction, but is not yet known for the empirical data. In such a case we shall simply accept the verification as successful but weak.

THE SOCIAL LEARNING THEORY

This theory states that religious behaviour, beliefs and experiences are simply part of the culture, and are regularly transmitted from generation to generation, in the same way as any other customs. This view has of course been widely held, and there is much obvious evidence for it, for example the fact that children reared in different parts of the world tend to acquire the local religious beliefs. To some extent we assume this theory when we talk of the different religions of different countries, for it is assumed that these are relatively unchanging and will persist in time. This is clearly a 'same-level' explanation, postulating that religion is learnt by the same processes of socialization as are other attitudes and beliefs.

It is not necessary to make any specific predictions to test this theory, since the whole chapter on Environmental Factors provides a mass of direct evidence in its favour. What the detailed evidence does for us here is to show that the old theory was correct, and to show in detail how this learning takes place. It is found for example that children acquire much the same beliefs as their parents, particularly if they like them and continue to live at home: the same is true, to much the same extent, of attitudes on political and other matters. Religious attitudes and beliefs are modified by membership of educational and other social groups, in the same way that other attitudes are affected. There is some evidence that the content of mystical experiences depends on the beliefs which are held beforehand (pp. 112–61), and that the stigmata have occurred as a result of suggestion in hysterical personalities—no one experienced this before St. Francis, though several hundred have done so since that time (Thurston, 1951).

It is possible to specify the theory more by deciding to which religious groups it is most applicable, and which situations of social learning are most relevant. It was found that people who had been to Sunday School did not experience sudden conversions (p. 43). From this it follows that the learning experiences in extreme Protestant groups take place later, and at revival meetings, while in more Catholic groups the learning occurs earlier—in the home and at Sunday School. It was found that authoritarians tended to accept their parental views more often than others (p. 41); since authoritarians tend to belong to Catholic-type churches, this supports the previous conclusion that Protestants learn their religion later. However, religious views seem to be established in children by the age 12–18 (pp. 59–65), apart from subsequent systematic age changes. This is a rather later age than in the case of racial attitudes, and earlier than the age by which political attitudes are formed. This all supports the idea that religious behaviour and beliefs are partly the result of the usual social learning processes.

While there is a good deal of evidence in support of the social learning theory, its limitations are obvious. In the first place it cannot account for any of the very considerable individual differences in religious activity within the culture—variations due to age, sex, personality and social class in particular. This is because the theory shows how religion is passed on but does not show the motivational forces maintaining it—behaviour is not learned unless a need is satisfied, though several different ways of satisfying the same need may be learned. The theory obviously provides one important postulate of a more complete account.

The other important limitation of the theory is that it predicts, if anything, that all religious movements will remain unchanged by time; it cannot account for the initiation of new movements or for the decline of old ones. Another approach is to use the model of the epidemic—the right kind of leader under the right conditions puts a number of people into a certain state, the number affected grows at a certain rate and finally dies down (Penrose, 1952). There is some similarity between the emergence of new sects and epidemics, except that some sects settle down to a final steady state instead of disappearing, while others change their whole character and become denominations; it is difficult to draw any concrete predictions from this theory.

RELIGION AS A RESPONSE TO FRUSTRATION

The theory that religion is some kind of response or adaptation to frustration has been put forward more often than any other theory about the psychological basis of religion. Freud, in his book, *Civilisation and its Discontents* (1939), suggests that religion is one possible mode of adaptation to the frustration of the basic instincts due to civilization, and to privations resulting from natural catastrophes. Karl Marx similarly maintained that 'religion is the opium of the people'—i.e. that the frustrations of the working class are alleviated by religion. Different writers have suggested different kinds of frustration: economic and sexual deprivation have been postulated, as well as the frustrations of loneliness ('social needs'). The theory can be stated alternatively by saying that religion is motivated by one or more of these needs; however, it may be presumed that religious behaviour would only occur if the normal outlet was prevented, hence this form of the theory is equivalent to the first. A variety of psychological mechanisms can be postulated to link frustration with the religious behaviour: for example that beliefs are a substitutive fantasy, or that prayer is a magical means of producing desired results.

In this section we shall examine evidence to throw light on the basic hypothesis that frustration leads to increased religious activity. The question will be put in the following way: Are there any groups of people for whom the frustration of any need leads to greater religious activity?

How can this question be answered? The simplest way would be to compare two groups of people of which one group is more frustrated than the other, and to see if this group is the more religious. The difficulty with this method of verification is that it is so hard to tell which people *are* the most frustrated—if some people have a less active social life than others it does not follow that they are frustrated, they may simply have a less developed need for social life. This is particularly true of secondary, non-biological needs which are largely acquired during socialization and therefore vary widely in strength amongst different people. Another possibility is that they are not so much frustrated by external circumstances as inhibited by the internal restrictions of the 'super-ego' or some such mechanism. This leads to a rather different theory—that religion is an outcome of conflict between the super-ego and the instincts; this will be considered later. We can be certain that a lowered rate of response, e.g. reduced sexual activity, is due to frustration only if frustrating circumstances are imposed externally. The best way of testing the theory would be to carry out a large scale experiment in which one group is severely frustrated in some way while a matched control group is not, but this of course is impracticable. Sometimes, however, external events—such as wars, economic changes and disasters—do take place in a way which makes it quite clear that the frustration is externally imposed.

There is a second method of verification. If a form of religious belief is an adjustment to frustration, then that belief should act as a kind of substitute so that it can satisfy the frustrated need in fantasy. It might be possible to carry out a comparable type of verification on ritual practices: however it seems likely that the psychological mechanisms producing such rituals are rather complex, so that it may not prove possible to recognize the originally frustrated need in them.

A third method of testing the theory has been used by Welford (1947). Subjects were asked to place six situations which were described in rank order for emotional involvement, frustration and the likelihood of their praying in the situation. The latter correlated on average ·59 with frustration, ·51 with emotional involvement; partial correlations came to ·47 and ·33 respectively. It seems that frustration is one factor in prayer, emotional involvement being a quite independent one. Furthermore, it emerged that some subjects were most likely to pray in the frustrating situation, others in the emotionally involving ones. This is a very interesting finding in that it suggests that the frustration theory is applicable to certain people only, and that different explanations must be postulated for others. There is, however, no more research using this method, and the rest of the discussion will be confined to the first two methods of verification.

Economic and Social Status Deprivation. Although economic needs are socially acquired, they are widely shared in Western society—as is shown by the almost universal attempt to make more money, either by individual or by group action. Similarly, the need for social status, although varying widely between different people in strength, is agreed by sociologists to be well-nigh universal. Although these two needs exist quite independently, it is not possible to separate their effects with the data available, since status and wealth are highly correlated, and so they will be treated together.

(1) The most effective test of the hypothesis that religion is due to economic deprivation can be made by a study of the level of religious activity at different points in the trade cycle—since this can be regarded as externally imposed. As was stated earlier (pp. 137–9) the major denominations in Britain and America were little affected by the depression of the 1930's, showing if anything a slight decline. During the economic boom in America since the war there has been a steady increase in religious activity of all kinds; while it is possible that prosperity brings its own frustrations, there is no objective evidence for this. For the major denominations, then, economic frustration does not produce greater religious activity, but to some extent the reverse. It has sometimes been maintained (e.g. by Boisen, 1955) that the minor Protestant sects grew during the depression. It is true that they increased in membership over this period, but they have been increasing rapidly in all periods since 1900, so that there is no unique connexion with economic deprivation here (pp. 138–9).

(2) If religion is a result of economic or social status deprivation, it follows that the working classes should be more religious —though the verification is less satisfactory since the direction of causation is unclear. As shown earlier (pp. 129–31), there is a slight tendency for the middle classes to be most religious in America, and the upper and middle classes in Great Britain. This confirms the previous finding that for the main religious groups there is a small relationship between religious activity

and economic prosperity rather than frustration. If the small sects are considered separately, a very clear relationship appears—their membership is largely amongst the very poor (pp. 130–3).* This could be the result of social status frustration rather than of economic—particularly as there is no clear relationship with the business cycle. It might also be due to the deliberate pursuit of poverty on the part of these groups, as is the case with monastic orders; this seems unlikely in view of the tendency for these sects to change their whole character as their members move upwards in the socal scale (p. 34). We may conclude that so far as the main religious groups are concerned, economic frustration is not relevant—being if anything related to religious *in*activity. However, for the minor Protestant sects there is clear evidence that membership in them is related to either economic or social frustration.

Can the conclusion that the sects are the product of economic or social frustration be supported by means of the other method of verification—i.e. by seeing if their beliefs are compensatory? Clark (1949) summarizes the common characteristics of 200 American sects and concludes that their beliefs *are* compensatory: (1) their belief in the speedy ending of this world and the coming of the next where the rich shall be cast down and the humble and meek raised up, (2) their puritan morality in which a virtue is made of frugality, humility and industry, while luxuries and wordly amusements are vices, (3) the stress on simplicity of worship and opposition to expensive equipment: the Churches of Christ opposed missionary activity because of the cost involved, (4) the Church of the Nazarene openly states that its mission is to the poor, others to negroes. As Clark says, it is curious that none of these bodies is interested in social reform. It seems that there are two opposed types of response to economic and social status deprivation—an other-worldly fantasy response, and a left-wing political action response. We may conclude that there is good evidence for the truth of our theory in the case of the small sects.

(3) It is possible that many people get adjusted to their economic and social status and only experience frustration or satisfaction when it changes. Lenski (1953) found that people who had moved downwards in social status compared with

*With the exception of Christian Scientists.

their parents were more interested in religion than those who had kept the same position, and that the latter were more interested than those who had moved upwards. Since changes of prosperity in the business cycle produce no general change in the level of religious activity it is likely that Lenski's results reflect changes of status rather than changes of prosperity. Unfortunately no differential analysis of beliefs is available here.

(4) On the present hypothesis underprivileged minority groups should be more religious than other people. It is the case that American negroes for example are considerably more religious than the main population (pp. 133–4), and it should be noted that their religion tends to be of the small sect and ecstatic type. The Kingdom of Father Divine is clearly a frustration-inspired movement in view of its aims which are to improve the social and economic status of the American negroes (Cantril, 1941). However, this is to some extent a political movement—which tries to bring about its ends by social action. It is common for political groups to develop in response to frustration; our problem is whether this is also true of religious movements—which try to bring about their ends by means of prayer, belief and ceremony.

(5) Nottingham (1954) suggests that the beliefs associated with the Hindu caste system developed to ease its stresses: it is believed that a person's position in the system is merited by his performance in previous incarnations, and social discontent is averted by these beliefs. This theory, that beliefs are generated to relieve the frustrations of the social and political order, has some support: Nottingham gives other examples and Kardiner (1941) traces the development of Jewish-Christian beliefs in these terms. However, these are all *ex post facto* interpretations and are weaker verifications than the statistical ones given earlier. Similar considerations apply to Pfister's very interesting demonstration (1948) that the Jewish-Christian community has always become more ritualistic in times of stress. Other parts of Pfister's thesis will be examined later.

The theory has more commonly been held in another, less easily verifiable, form. It is maintained that many people go to church 'for social reasons', or 'to maintain their respectability'. Clearly such a theory is only tenable in a community where it *is* respectable to go to church, i.e. where the upper classes attend most frequently; as shown above, England is to some extent like this, but America is not (pp. 129–31).

(1) The clearest prediction from this is that the upper classes should be relatively less active in private religious activities: the English surveys show that class differences in private prayer are rather less than for church attendance, though in the same direction; differences of belief and attitude show little variation with social class. There is thus a certain amount of confirmation for the prediction.

(2) It can be deduced that people with a greater need for status should go to church more. We may assume that needs are stronger among those deprived of the appropriate gratification —in this case those of low social status. However, these people go to church *least*, so that the theory is directly opposed by the evidence here.

Frustration of Social Needs. In addition to the need for social status, people have a 'gregarious' need for the company of others and the membership of social groups.

(1) The most clear-cut test of the hypothesis is provided by the case of widows, since they are suffering from a major frustration of social needs which is externally imposed. While sexual frustration may also be involved, widowhood generally occurs at an age when the sexual side of marriage is less important. In fact the religious activity of widows is greater than that of married people (pp. 123–4), though this may be partly due to age differences. Applying the second method of verification, we find that widows believe more in the after-life, believe that they will rejoin their loved ones there, and include a high percentage of spiritualists (p. 124). There seems fairly good evidence that the hypothesis is correct in this case.

(2) Areas which are socially disorganized—which suffer from 'anomie'—should be more religious on this hypothesis. There is little material here, but it was concluded in an earlier section (pp. 136–7) that there is no evidence for any relationship between religion and social disorganization.

(3) On the present hypothesis, people go to church primarily for the social contacts. This cannot generally be true in view of the great frequency with which people say private prayers and read the Bible, or at any rate report that they do. It may how-

ever be true of certain groups of people that they go to church for such social reasons. If there is any truth in the hypothesis, it would be expected that churches with more organized social activities would attract a larger following. It is not known whether or not this is so, but it is known that many American churches organize an amazing variety of purely secular activities (Douglass, 1926). This may well be one of the reasons for the recent growth of interest in religion in America, where there is now much more religious activity than in Great Britain (pp. 35–8).

To conclude, there is good evidence that the religious activity of widows is related to social frustration; possibly social needs are of wider importance, but the evidence is insufficient to say.

Frustration of the Sexual Instinct. This has often been proposed as the basis for religion. It is very difficult to obtain a clear verification for this hypothesis on the first method, although several indirect tests are possible. A difficulty here is that reduced sexual activity may be due to *internal* inhibition by the super-ego, as well as to glandular deficiency.

(1) If the hypothesis is correct, people with a lower level of sexual activity should be more religious. This is certainly the case (pp. 121–3), though it could be because the Church discourages some kinds of sexual behaviour. The evidence is not clear on the last point: although religious people are particularly low on forbidden forms of sexual activity, they are low on other kinds as well. The results are as predicted by the hypothesis in question, but could be explained in other ways.

(2) Unmarried people should be more religious than married, since it may be assumed that in general their opportunities for sexual outlet are less. Social surveys show that single people are slightly more religious than married (pp. 123–4); again this is consistent with the hypothesis but could be explained in other ways.

(3) It has been suggested that the heightened religious activity of adolescence is due to the lack of adequate outlet for the awakening sexual instinct. The true situation is rather complex, and it is doubtful if it can provide any support for the hypothesis. There is no evidence of an *increase* of religious

activity during adolescence, it is simply that young people decide for or against their childhood faith during this period (pp. 59–65). There is in fact a decline of belief from the age of 12 and of church attendance from 18. There is probably a good deal of sexual frustration from about 15 onwards, since the sexual instinct is then at full strength, and no socially acceptable outlet is available. It should also be remembered that old age is the most religious time of life—when the sexual instinct is greatly weakened. It will be argued later that sudden conversions during adolescence may be due to guilt feelings which come to a height during this time.

(4) Turning to the second means of verification, the clearest instance of a sexual content to religious activities is provided by some of the classical saints and mystics. As has been demonstrated by Leuba (1925) and Thouless (1924) many of the writings are full of scarcely-disguised sexual symbolism. When we consider that these people had no overt sexual satisfaction at all, it seems very likely that frustration or internal inhibition of this instinct is partly responsible for their religious activities. Thouless (op. cit., p. 133) regards the great emphasis placed on chastity as evidence of the sexual basis of religion. It will be used in a later section in support of the theory that religion is due to conflict between the sexual instinct and the super-ego.

To conclude this section on the sexual frustration hypothesis, there is evidence in the case of the mystics that frustration or internal inhibition is operative; the greater religious activity of unmarried people and those with little sexual activity also supports one or other of these theories.

Fear of Death. Anthropologists like Malinoswki (1925) have stressed the functions of religion in helping those facing death to adjust to the situation, as well as in helping those who are bereaved. This can be regarded as an anticipated frustration in so far as all the satisfactions of this life are about to be ended, and it is uncertain what is to follow.

(1) It would be expected that people will be progressively more religious as they get older. As has been shown above (pp. 67–70), there is an increasing amount of religious activity from the age of 30 onwards. It has been found that the index which is most affected by age is belief in an after-life—100 per

cent of people over 90 were certain of an after-life in one survey, although not all expressed a favourable attitude towards religion, or engaged in religious practices (p. 68). Similarly, the number of people who said they went to church 'for reassurance of immortality' increased progressively after the age of 30 (p. 69). All this goes to confirm the view that the rise in religious belief after 30 is related to fear of death.

(2) The finding that for old people those who are not religious are rather less well adjusted (p. 104) may also be cited in support of the hypothesis.

(3) It would be predicted that people exposed to great danger would become more religious. Surveys of soldiers in World War II showed that about three-quarters were greatly helped by prayer, particularly those who had been exposed to the greatest danger, and who experienced the most anxiety; it was also found that ex-servicemen were more religious than before, especially if they had been in action. These men were more religious in the sense of believing more in God and being more concerned with religious questions, but their church attendance was not affected (pp. 49–51).

Illness. Being incurably ill is for most people a particularly severe form of frustration, and it might be expected on the frustration theory that a religious response would develop.

(1) It would be expected in the first place that sick people would be more religious. Wilson (1955) reports that Christian Science congregations contain a large number of crippled and deformed people: in conformity with the Christian Science be-belief that all bodies are perfect, members ignore these defects in one another, and make only the most perfunctory inquiries after their health. Wilson reports an American analysis of 500 testimonies: 93 per cent of these discussed the maintenance of health, and 50 per cent of people said that they had joined the movement to cure an illness.

(2) It would be expected that special religious beliefs and practices would be developed to deal with illness. In fact there are many such movements, and these have been surveyed by Weatherhead (1951). The partial success of all these movements is no doubt due to the alleviation of psychosomatic complaints by suggestion. It is interesting to note that although about 3 per

cent of visitors to Lourdes are helped (McComb, 1928), the majority of these cures are not counted by the Catholic authorities as 'miracles', which are said to occur about once every two years.

*   *   *   *   *

This concludes the discussion of frustration. Perhaps the most important conclusion is that most religious behaviour and belief is not a response to frustration at all. The cases which fulfil the empirical expectations of the frustration theory are as follows:

- (a) minor Protestant sects (economic and social status deprivation),
- (b) widows (social need deprivation),
- (c) mystics (sexual deprivation),
- (d) the aged, soldiers in action (fear of death),
- (e) the chronically ill (the frustrations of illness and fear of death).

RELIGION AND CONFLICT

The two theories now to be discussed postulate that religion is a product not of external frustration but of conflict between two parts of the personality, in particular between the super-ego (or conscience) and the instincts. Although five of Freud's books and a number of papers are concerned with religion, he did not develop a single unified theory: the two theories to be discussed here, like others to be discussed later, have been developed by later psychoanalytic writers from particular parts of his writing on religion. The central core of psychoanalytic theory has also been extended since Freud, and we shall take the basic theory not from Freud but from the later monumental statement due to Fenichel (1945). Most of the theorizing has of course not been verified in terms of experimental and statistical data, indeed the theory was never put forward with such ideas in mind. There have been a variety of attempts to test psychoanalytic hypotheses against such empirical data. We shall here suggest another method of verification: the theories about religion will be tested by seeing how far predictions derived from them can be confirmed against various kinds of statistical data.

The first conflict theory was put forward by Flugel in his book *Man, Morals and Society* (1945), and postulates that the

154

super-ego is 'projected' on to God. The basic theory of the super-ego can be summarized briefly as follows: the child is punished by its parents either physically or by the withdrawal of love for indulging in certain behaviour, and it experiences anxiety when it does so because of the anticipated punishment. The child identifies itself with the parents and wishes to be like them and conform to their demands. Thus the parental requirements become 'internalized', and the child now feels guilty even if the parents are absent: the psychological mechanism which represents the parental demands is called the super-ego. The super-ego is harsh and irrational because aggression towards the parents is redirected on to the self; this is particularly likely to happen when the parents are kind but frustrating in subtle ways. When physical punishment is used, children feel more able to express their frustration in outward aggression.

The super-ego is likely to come into conflict with instinctual desires, particularly sexual and aggressive desires. Flugel's theory (1945) is that this conflict is relieved by 'projection' of the super-ego which now appears as God. Projection, or externalization, is a defence mechanism: an internal process or property is reacted to as if it were outside the individual. For example the super-ego can be projected on to a doctor, teacher, leader or priest; the repressive demands of the super-ego are then thought to be prohibitions which are imposed by the person in question, who is felt to be coercing and looking down on the subject. Alternatively, the instinctive desires can be projected on to groups of people such as the Jews or negroes, who are then thought to be highly sexed and aggressive. The gains for the individual are that the conflict is reduced through being no longer an inner one, while he feels that he can deal with the situation by overt action, instead of by changing himself (cf. Horney, 1946). On Flugel's formulation a more radical type of projection is postulated, in which the super-ego is projected on to the Universe as a God, and the instinctive desires similarly as the Devil (Flugel, op. cit.; Fenichel, 1945).

Several later psychoanalytic writers mention the function of religion in relieving guilt feelings (e.g. Pfister, 1948). Some people have more guilt feelings than others, and it may be supposed that these will be the more religious, on the present hypothesis. Mackinnon and Rosenzweig (in Murray, 1938) carried out a very interesting series of experiments which are relevant here. They distinguished between extrapunitive, intropunitive and impunitive people, according to whether, when faced with frustration, they blamed and displayed aggression towards other people, towards themselves, or not at all. Mackinnon found that people who did not violate the experimental instructions when tempted to do so were intropunitive both in what they said and in overt actions (such as scratching themselves); these people often felt guilty in everyday life, and had been disciplined in childhood by loss of love rather than by physical punishment. Rosenzweig found that intropunitives were not outwardly aggressive, but showed signs of strong superego conflict (cf. Flugel, 1945). We may conclude that intropunitives have a strong super-ego, and experience guilt feelings: on the present theory they should be more religious.

The two inhibition theories have now been stated. Both theories postulate a conflict between the instincts and the superego as the basis of religion, and this hypothesis will be verified first. Later the separate predictions of the two theories will be considered. The tests which can be made of the first hypothesis are as follows:

(1) If the instincts are opposed by the super-ego in religious people, this should result in a diminution of the forbidden instinctive activity. Sexual activity is lower for devout religious people, whether Catholics, Protestants or Jews (pp. 121–3); this was mentioned in connexion with the frustration theory, but it is likely that sexual behaviour is prevented by internal rather than external restraints. Confirmation of another kind is provided by Unwin's study (1934) of eighty primitive societies: he rated each society for the degree of restriction on sexual behaviour and for the development of religion; the two variables were found to be highly correlated with each other. Aggressive behaviour too would be expected to be lower in religious people: research shows that regular churchgoers are less delinquent, though this is not true of church *members* or those who merely hold orthodox beliefs (pp. 96–99).

(2) Since neuroses may be caused by conflicts between the super-ego and the instincts, we should expect religious people to be more neurotic on the inhibition theory. In fact *young* religious people are more neurotic than young non-religious

people, but the reverse is true for old people (pp. 102–7). This suggests that the inhibition theory may only apply to young people—whose instincts are stronger, and who still retain the parental demands in their super-ego.

(3) If religious behaviour is derived from the super-ego in some way, religion should have an irrational 'super-ego' quality about it. There are several ways in which this proves to be true. Funk (1956) discovered that a majority of students thought that they were not as strict in their religion as they ought to be, and wished that they were perfectly sure that religion was true. Secondly religion always has an ethical flavour, in which powerful moral demands are made, and sin is condemned. Thirdly, God is often perceived as a forbidding punishing figure: many Christians hold an Old Testament view of God, despite the teachings of the New. Religious people are more authoritarian than non-religious people, and authoritarians perceive God very much in this awesome way (pp. 90–91). As will be shown presently, there are important differences between religious groups in this respect.

We have now established some evidence for the theory that religion is a product of conflict between the super-ego and the instincts. The verification of the remaining parts of the two inhibition theories can be simplified by extending them slightly. I shall postulate that the projection of the super-ego theory applies primarily to Roman Catholics, while the relief of guilt theory applies primarily to Protestants. It is not being suggested that the mechanism apply exclusively but that there is a difference of emphasis between these religious groups. We shall find that the theories work rather better if these groups are somewhat redefined. With Catholics we shall include members of similar Protestant bodies—like the Lutheran Church and the Church of England as well as religious conservatives in general. By Protestants we mean to refer to the main 'nonconformist' denominations such as Methodists, Presbyterians and Baptists; small Protestant sects are not included, nor are Unitarians, Quakers or Congregationalists. The reasons for this classification will be clear later (pp. 171–7). The verifications of the two inhibition theories, postulated to apply as described, and apart from the verifications already made, are as follows:

(1) If the relief of guilt theory applies primarily to Protestants,

they should be more intropunitive than Catholics. The evidence shows that Protestants have a higher rate of suicide than Catholics (pp. 99–100); Durkheim (1898) thought this was due to the supposedly less cohesive social grouping of Protestant communities, but that is extremely speculative; no doubt the Catholic teaching on suicide is also partly responsible. Catholics have a higher rate of delinquency (pp. 96–99), which also supports the hypothesis. Studies of psychotic patients show that Protestants often have ideas of sin and unworthiness (Farr & How, 1932). Protestant doctrine and practice are also in line with the theory: Protestants are more concerned with sin and salvation, and new members must repent of their sins and believe that they are saved. It might be thought that the Catholic practice of confession showed that Catholics are intropunitive. It will be shown later that Catholics project the super-ego on to the priesthood: Catholics can thus obtain forgiveness for the guilt feelings which they do have in this way whereas Protestants with their more internalized super-ego cannot.

(2) Authoritarians are extrapunitive and they also tend to use projection as a defence mechanism (Adorno, et al., 1950). It might be expected that Catholics would score higher on this trait than Protestants. This is the case, although Protestants too score considerably higher than non-religious people (pp. 87–91). Authoritarians accept a hierarchical style of organization and leadership—an important difference between Catholics and Protestants. If the super-ego can be projected on to God, it could even more readily be projected on to the Pope or other ecclesiastical authorities, which may also go to account for the Catholic acceptance of a religious hierarchy. Dreger (1952), using projective methods, found a higher need for dependence among religious conservatives; this supports the personality difference postulated here. Finally, Catholics and other religious conservatives are high in racial prejudice (pp. 83–85), suggesting both extrapunitiveness and projectivity—on the scapegoat theory of prejudice.

(3) What does the present theory predict about sex differences? Women are less authoritarian than men (Adorno et al 1950), and there is some evidence that they are more intropunitive: Bernard (1949) found this using the Rosenzweig Picture

Frustration Test; Blum (1949) found the same using the Blackie test; women are less delinquent* and less aggressive in various situations. We should expect therefore that women would prefer Protestantism to Catholicism, and we find that there are 25–55 per cent more women in Protestant bodies, compared with about 10 per cent more for Catholics (pp. 76–78), while the Eastern Orthodox churches have more men than women.

(4) Protestants, it has been suggested, are religious as the result of internalized motivations connected with the super-ego. Catholics do not have such an internalized super-ego; as authoritarians they are more susceptible to external social influence, and it seems likely that they may project the super-ego on to the priesthood. In other words, Protestants are religious through inner motivations, Catholics through social pressure. It follows that Protestants should engage more in private as opposed to public prayer, though of course more pressure for attendance is exerted by Catholic than by Protestant clergy. A statistical comparison is provided by two British surveys: Odham's Press (1947) inquired about frequency of church attendance, the British Institute of Public Opinion (1950) asked 'Apart from children, does anyone in your home pray regularly?' The results are shown in Table 41.

TABLE 41. Public/Private Religion and Denomination

	Weekly attendance%	Pray regularly%
Roman Catholics	52	68
Nonconformists	14	43
Church of England	8	48

(From Odhams Press (1947), B.I.P.O. (1950))

It can be seen that the relative amount of private prayer is far greater for the Protestant denominations. Sex differences are greater for private religious activities than for public (pp. 71–76), as would be expected from the stronger super-ego of women and their tendency towards Protestantism. Similarly, Blum (1949) found that men have an externalized super-ego

---

*However, they also have a smaller suicide rate, showing that there are further complexities to the problem.

which is sensitive to social pressures: women are more concerned with internal deprivations and fear of loss of love from internalized figures. Crutchfield (1957) in a long series of experiments found that conformity in men was correlated with anxiety (presumably over social rejection), while in women it was correlated with measures of emotional restriction, or repression.*

(5) Gradual conversions, it was suggested previously, are probably due to social learning. Sudden conversions, however, may be explicable on the present theory. Sudden conversions do take place in groups which stress guilt and salvation, often at emotional mass meetings (pp. 53, 62). Can the theory also explain why such conversions should occur during adolescence, at around the ages 14–17? Thouless (1924) suggested that adolescent conversion is due to the 'sublimation' of the recently awakened, but suppressed, sexual instinct. Perhaps guilt over adolescent expressions of sexuality makes young people particularly receptive to this type of religion. Starbuck (1899) found that a number of his subjects had guilt feelings of this kind; Clark (1929) found that 55 per cent of his sudden converts suffered from a sense of sin, compared with 8½ per cent for the total sample of converts; 57 per cent of the sudden converts experienced subsequent joy, compared with 14 per cent for the total.

* * * * *

We can take the problem a little further by considering the position of small Protestant sects. It has already been shown how they come into being under conditions of social and economic frustration (pp. 147–50), and later may develop into orthodox Protestant denominations. In several ways, they can be regarded as representing an extreme degree of Protestantism—i.e. a further point along the Catholic–Protestant dimension. In particular they place even more emphasis on sin, salvation and conversion, they have no ordained clergy or ecclesiastical line of authority, there is much emphasis on evangelism, and their services are simple, enthusiastic and non-ritualistic. We might expect then that they would score even further away from

---

*However it was found in this and other studies that women are more amenable to social pressure, a fact which requires further explanation.

Catholics than do the main Protestant denominations on various indices.

(1) On authoritarianism the sects are considerably lower than other Protestants, and they score even lower than non-religious people (p. 84).

(2) The proportion of women is rather higher than for the other denominations—typically there are about twice as many women as men (p. 76).

(3) Sudden conversion is more common in these bodies, and in revivalistic phases of Protestantism.

There is no evidence concerning the intropunitiveness or private religious activities of sect members, but the above three findings confirm the application of the reduction of guilt theory to sects, classified as a further degree of Protestantism.

To summarize this section, there is considerable evidence that religion is due to conflict between the super-ego and the instincts, and that the projection of the super-ego theory applies primarily to Catholics, the reduction of guilt theory to Protestants, especially extreme Protestant sects. In fact the two theories between them account for no fewer than twenty statistical findings about religious activity, together with seven differences of organization or doctrine.

THE THEORY THAT GOD IS A FANTASY FATHER-FIGURE

The Future of an Illusion (1927) is Freud's best known book on religion, partly because of its atheistic conclusions. However, we are concerned with Freud's psychology, not his theology, though it is the theology which has aroused most comment. In this book, as well as in *Civilisation and its Discontents* (1939) Freud puts forward the frustration hypothesis: religion is a pleasant illusion in response to (*a*) the frustrations of 'Nature' with its uncontrollable catastrophes, its 'destructive forces from the outer world', and the decay of the body; (*b*) the suppression of instinctive desires—sexual, aggressive and egoistic—by the forces of civilization, which are assisted by the internalization of these restraints in the super-ego; (*c*) the relative deprivation of the working classes by other sections of society; finally, and curiously, he suggests that suffering is easier than pleasure which can only be obtained from the momentary satisfaction of pent-up

needs. This is an elaborate version of the frustration hypothesis, for which the general evidence has been reviewed above.
It will be noted that sexual frustration plays a small part in the
theory, and the sexual instinct is said to be partly suppressed by
the super-ego. Later psychoanalytic thought has placed less
emphasis on external frustration, and more on conflict within
the personality.

In response to these frustrations the person regresses to a
period when he was dependent on his father for protection, and
forms the illusion that a Father in Heaven is protecting him:
Nature is endowed with fatherly characteristics. However the
child was ambivalent towards the real father—i.e. was dependent on him for love and protection but also feared his wrath—
so God also is seen as one who must be feared and propitiated,
but who will protect. The reason which Freud gives for the
original father being feared is that the boy has a residue of guilt
towards his father, over the Oedipus situation, in which the
small boy had a quasi-sexual interest in his mother. (Another
explanation, within the Freudian system, might be simply that
the boy had internalized the father's actual punishments and
restrictions.) The function of prayer on this theory is that it
affords a magical way of influencing nature—'a way of con-
trolling the real world by the wish world' (1933).

We now turn to ways of verifying the theory as stated here.

(1) If God is a projection of a father-image, then God should
be perceived as being like a father. It is true that God is often
thought of and spoken of as a Father; on the other hand many
people do not think of God as resembling a human being at all.
In Leuba's study (1921) of 900 students, 7 per cent had an
image of God as a real human being, 27 per cent as symbolized
by a human being, while over half had no image of God at all;
however 82 per cent of the women and 56 per cent of the men
thought of God as personal; it is possible that most of the 70 per
cent who believed in God did think of him as a person even if
some had no image. The issue is difficult because the idea people
hold of God must be formed primarily as a result of social learning; we must turn to individual differences between groups
equally exposed to social learning, but differing in other ways,
to make a crucial test. If God is a projected father-image, then
a person's idea of and attitude towards God would be like his

idea of and attitude towards his own father. This could be tested, but it would be difficult, since the unconscious ideas and attitudes would have to be included, and these would have to be obtained by psychoanalytic or projective methods.

There is some evidence that children between the ages 3–6 tend to think of God as like their own father (p. 59). This does not really support Freud's theory, though it might be thought to lend some support for Bovet's theory (1928) that at the age of 4 the child discovers that the parents are not omnipotent and creates a fantasy figure which is. A simpler explanation is that God is described to children by means of analogies as a kind of father or king.

(2) If a person regresses in the face of frustration to needing a protecting father, he will not create an imaginary father if he already has a real protecting father. Children who leave home early, or whose father dies, should develop religious beliefs. This may explain the frequency of adolescent conversions— they may take place after leaving home, or possibly they may occur when the real father ceases to be satisfactory in some way. Should children who have never had a father be atheists? It is not clear from Freudian writings whether the need for a protecting father is the result of social processes or is innately biological, so that no clear deduction follows here.

(3) Children are protected not only by the father, but also by the mother; why then should not a female deity, or indeed a whole family circle, be projected on to nature? As Jung and others have pointed out, other religions commonly do have such deities, and it may well prove the most important contribution of psychoanalysis to the study of religion to have pointed out the resemblance between Holy Families and human families. It is outside the scope of the present book to inquire into the sociological conditions under which a particular deity or set of deities is believed in. In Western society God is traditionally male, though Catholics pay considerable attention to the Virgin Mary. On the Freudian theory, children are more concerned with the opposite sexed parent; from this it follows that women should be more religious than men, if God is traditionally male. Catholicism ought to have more appeal for men, because of the Virgin Mary, who may act as a mother-figure. In Protestant churches, women are 25–55 per cent more active

than men, while in the Roman Catholic and Eastern Orthodox churches the sexes are nearly equally represented. (pp 76–78). These findings give some support to the present formulation.

(4) The Oedipal part of the theory explains why God is feared by men; it does not explain why a male God should be feared by women. People who have not resolved their Oedipus complex should fear God more, but would not necessarily be more religious. The usual theory is that women do not succeed in resolving their Oedipus complex so well—since men are motivated to do so by fear of castration (Fenichel, 1945, p. 108). However, Blum (1949) in his work using the 'Blackie' projection test found that *men* had more severe Oedipal conflicts. If this is so, then men should perceive God as a punishing figure more than women. Men score higher than women on authoritarianism, and authoritarians tend to perceive God in this way (Adorno, *et al.*, 1950).

This completes the discussion of the father-figure theory. The higher proportion of men in the Catholic church, and the greater authoritarianism of men, give limited support to the theory. Several other tests are suggested, but some involve dubious measurements and others dubious deductions. It appears that this theory is not easily verifiable, which is the same as saying that it is not empirically very fruitful.

THE OBSESSIONAL NEUROSIS THEORY

Freud (1907) put forward the suggestion that ritualistic religion was a kind of group equivalent of obsessional neurosis. It is important to be clear what kind of theory this is, for that affects the method of verification to be applied. The theory is a 'same level' theory: in other words it is a theory which attempts to explain a phenomenon by classifying it with another better known one (pp. 141–2). The theory would be confirmed if it were shown that empirical conditions producing obsessional neuroses also produce ritualistic religion. This is not the kind of procedure which has been used in any of the discussions of this theory. Freud (op. cit.) pointed to a number of *descriptive similarities* between obsessional neuroses and religious ritual, and Reik (1951) has considerably elaborated upon this. Philp (1956) has opposed the theory by pointing to differences between the two phenomena. In our view, these considerations are totally irrelevant.

However, there seems to be some measure of agreement between these writers about the similarities and differences between rituals and obsessions, so we will summarize these briefly in order to clarify the theory. (a) The psychoanalytic theory of obsessional neurosis is that obsessions are distorted symbolic versions either of instinctive desires forbidden by the super-ego, or of the super-ego's prohibitions themselves. The obsessions and compulsions simultaneously allow some substitute gratification both of the desire and of its prohibition: Fenichel suggests pleasureless compulsive masturbation as an example of such a compromise (1945, p. 271). Reik (op. cit.) similarly traces the development of ideas about the Trinity as a compromise between ideas of filial rebellion and veneration for the father. (b) The neurotic's rituals have a compulsive character, in that he must carry them out conscientiously and experiences guilt if he fails to do so: this is to some extent true of religious rituals too. (c) In religion there are taboos—of Sunday work, food before communion, and so forth: neurotics also have things which they must avoid touching or thinking about. Flugel (1945) suggests that the taboo of the king in primitive religion, together with the rituals he must perform, serves the functions of honouring and protecting him, but at the same time of limiting his power and making his life a burden—another compromise mechanism. Reik (op. cit.) points out that the taboos surrounding religious dogma develop as a defence against scepticism: at the same time the dogma is developed in absurd detail, reflecting an underlying contempt for it. (d) The real conflict in neurotics becomes displaced on to trivial details and verbal matters; this is also the case with religion, where the dogmas and rituals become elaborated in enormous detail, minute parts of which may become the basis for schisms and persecutions.

So much for the similarities which have been claimed, now we turn to the differences. (a) The most important difference is that neurotic obsessions are individual, while religious rituals are collective actions of a social group, and are carried out in public. (b) Freud maintained (op. cit.) that whereas obsessional neurosis is due to inhibition of the sexual instinct, religious ritual is due to the suppression of egoistic and anti-social needs. Fenichel (op. cit.) however maintains that obsessionals often have conflicts about submission and rebellion, cruelty and gentleness, as a result of regression to the anal-sadistic stage of development.

This kind of psychoanalytic literature makes good reading, and the interpretations made and analogies drawn may be felt to be illuminating—but there is no evidence whatever that they are correct. It would be possible to devise an unlimited number of psychoanalytic interpretations of religious rituals and beliefs, but there would be no way of deciding which one was the right one. We turn now to possible verifications of the central proposition of the theory, that rituals and dogmas can be classified with obsessional neuroses.

(1) To verify the theory we should first establish the empirical conditions for obsessional neurosis and see if they are true of religion. Unfortunately these conditions are not sufficiently well known for us to be able to carry out the verification with any confidence. There is, however, some evidence that obsessional neuroses occur in people who (a) have a personality which is rigid, persistent, stingy, orderly and discipline-loving, and (b) are later exposed to stress. The second part has already been considered: what evidence is there that religious ritualists have the kind of personality described? Mayer-Gross and his associates (1955) say that obsessionals tend to be Presbyterians, Plymouth Brethren and Jesuits—i.e. groups stressing discipline rather than ritual. Catholics, who *are* ritualistic, do not have the obsessional personality: as authoritarians they are *less* obstinate than others (pp. 85–91).* (2) If the group ritual is a kind of alternative to an individual neurosis, it follows that religious ritualists should be less neurotic. While this is to some extent true of old people, the reverse is true for young people, especially Catholics (pp. 102–6). As the theory is primarily concerned with ritualistic religion, this evidence goes against it.

(3) From Freud's idea that ritualistic religion comes from the suppression of anti-social desires, it follows that Catholics and other ritualists should be less delinquent, which is not the

---

*It is Protestants who take the lead in capitalist activities (Weber 1904–5) which, in their preoccupation with money, would be connected in psychoanalytic theory with the anal (obsessional) personality type.

case (pp. 96–99). However, from the theory that obsessionals regress to the anal-sadistic stage it would be expected that ritualists would engage in crimes of violence. It is the case that Catholics are frequently involved in crimes of violence, while Protestants are more often concerned with sexual offences, and Jews with financial ones (p. 98). This supports the prediction for Catholics, while suggesting the important role of sexual repression for Protestants.

This completes the verification of the theory, and it can be seen that the evidence on the whole goes against it. The only positive evidence is the number of acts of violence of Catholic delinquents. Thus, despite certain descriptive similarities, it does not appear useful to classify religion as an obsessional neurosis.

COGNITIVE NEED THEORIES

What we shall call cognitive theories maintain that a major mechanism behind religious beliefs is a purely cognitive desire to understand. Bartlett (1932) originally postulated an 'effort after meaning' to account for the tendency for the organism to reduce objects to the simple and familiar when perceiving complex stimuli for very short exposures. Anthropologists sometimes maintain that primitive mythologies serve the cognitive purpose of explaining curious features of the environment, as well as giving an acceptable account of perennial human problems such as death (Piddington, 1950).

Some writers, while apparently offering a cognitive theory, are in fact putting forward a frustration theory, where the beliefs are of a compensatory type. Nottingham's theory that the belief of the Hindus in a caste system is due to a cognitive effort to make sense of an otherwise unacceptable situation is like this. Cantril (1941) proceeds similarly for the Kingdom of Father Divine and several non-religious movements: in fact it is not cognitive needs but needs for social status and a better standard of living which are involved, and Cantril is supporting the frustration theory.

The real question is, does the need to understand provide the motivational support for religious belief in the absence of other frustrations? Flower's theory (1927) is genuinely cognitive, though some of the supporting examples which he gives are instances of frustration. Flower postulates that religion is a fantasy which appears when the discriminations required by a situation are too difficult for the organism: the individual reacts by analogy rather than by responding to the actual situation.

To verify the cognitive theory, it is necessary to discover situations in which people are puzzled, unable to understand, or in Flower's version, unable to discriminate. These people should then be more religious.

(1) Flower actually suggests one way of testing his theory: a sheltered child is more likely to undergo an adolescent conversion. No evidence is available on this point. It would of course be a test for the cognitive theory in general, not just for Flower's version.

(2) Another group of people who would be expected to be cognitively puzzled are those who move to another social group of some kind. People who move up or down in the class system are in fact less and more religious respectively than those who stay put (pp. 148–9), and are not uniformly more religious as the theory predicts. It is not known whether emigrants are more religious than other people, but in any case too many other factors are involved here for this to provide a clear-cut test.

(3) Another way of approaching the problem is to look for groups of people who are obviously puzzled, and to see if they adopt religious beliefs as a solution of their cognitive difficulties. One such group is that of adolescents, who are very perplexed about cosmic questions, the meaning of life, and so forth. A few years earlier or later they may be none the wiser, but are not puzzled about these questions. Do adolescents adopt religious beliefs as a solution? The answer is that some do and some do not, but that many of them decide for or against religion during adolescence (pp. 59–65). It appears then that religious beliefs relieve the puzzles of *some* adolescents at least. There is however a widely-held explanation of adolescent perplexity which throws a different light on this. Adolescents are not primarily bothered about the 'meaning of life' but about their ambiguous social status, their emerging sexual instinct, their new responsibility—or any of the many problems of adjustment which face all adolescents. These problems are not wholly conscious, and

are projected instead into the realm of ideology. Thus the ostensibly cognitive needs may really be based on the need to resolve conflicts of a more basic nature. Thus if the adoption of religious beliefs does end an adolescent's puzzles, it may really be a deeper motivational puzzle which has been resolved.

(4) A second group of puzzled people are schizophrenics (pp. 107–9). When they are cured—usually by physical means—they may still wonder about the same problems to some extent, but the problems no longer matter to them. This in itself suggests that the purely cognitive side of the matter is unimportant. Do schizophrenics find a religious solution? In fact many are religious, though in a bizarre, individual kind of way: they may adopt beliefs similar to primitive myths, but with themselves as a central figure (pp. 107–11). It seems more probable that the beliefs like those of adolescents are projections of deeper motivations than the concern with genuine cognitive problems. Cronin (1934) describes a number of case-studies of patients apparently suffering from religious conflicts: he argues that their conflicts are really in other spheres and shows how these have been projected on to the religious plane.

(5) Scientific research workers are professionally faced with difficult cognitive problems. On the whole, scientists are rather less religious than academic people in the arts; furthermore, workers in the less developed, and hence more puzzling, sciences such as psychology are less religious than physicists and chemists. Of course, this is weak evidence, since the problems facing scientists do not readily admit of a religious solution, and scientists are people accustomed to the suspense of judgement.

(6) Some support may be provided for the cognitive theory by Thouless's interesting finding (1935) that people are more certain of the truth of religious propositions than of factual ones of the type 'Tigers are to be found in some parts of China'. Subjects recorded their agreement or disagreement with the items on a 7-point scale: judgements of the religious items showed a stronger tendency towards the two extremes of judgement—disbelief being as dogmatic as belief. Sanai (1952) in a similar study found a U-shaped distribution for political issues, but found a W-shaped one for religious items—a proportion of subjects opting for the mid-point. There could be various

interpretations of these results; one is that people must have a cognitive solution to these issues and opt for one extreme viewpoint or the other; on factual matters, suspension of judgement is more possible.

A rather different version of the cognitive theory has been put forward by Festinger (1955). He suggests that people are unsure about beliefs which cannot be checked against physical reality, and bolster up their beliefs by seeking social support for them. Interesting support for this theory is provided by his case-study of an end-of-the-world cult. This sect predicted the end of the world on three successive dates. After the first two failures the group increased its evangelistic activities—as would be predicted by theory but not by common sense. After the third fiasco the group did break up, however.

The effort after meaning, in the absence of other frustrations, does not seem to have much support in the empirical material as an explanation of religious phenomena. While puzzled adolescents and schizophrenics *are* more religious, other explanations seem more likely. Further tests could be devised, following Flower's suggestions. Festinger's theory that people need social support for their beliefs has a certain amount of evidence in its favour.

PHYSIOLOGICAL THEORIES

Most modern psychologists assume that behaviour of all kinds is mediated by physiological processes. The theories discussed so far have postulated complex processes like learning and the defence mechanisms which could take place only in the central nervous system: there are a number of other theories which have in common the supposition that religious phenomena spring from a 'lower level' of the physiological system—that is, that they come from the autonomic system, the contents of the blood-stream or elsewhere. In this section, we shall discuss the evidence for this hypothesis, and in doing so try to discover in detail what this physiological origin might be. Instead of making any specific predictions, which would be impossible with such a vague hypothesis, we shall simply examine the fields which provide some relevant evidence.

(1) The effects of drugs have been reviewed above (pp.

112–6). We concluded that mescaline, lysergic acid and similar substances produce vivid hallucinations, distortions of time perception, the feeling of being in touch with a deeper reality and depersonalization, apparently similar to mystical experiences. Some subjects who have been given these drugs have regarded their experiences as 'religious'. The Mexican tribes who take peyote have religious experiences which vary with the religious beliefs of the tribe: for example the Catholic tribes in Mexico have visions of the Virgin Mary. It was tentatively concluded that the experiences produced by certain drugs tend to be regarded as religious if those taking the drugs already possess a set of religious beliefs with which to interpret the experiences.

(2) The religion of psychotic patients was reviewed above (pp. 107–9), and it was concluded that about one in seven is preoccupied with bizarre self-referential religious ideas, including delusions, hallucinatory voices and mystical experiences: this occurs in all the main psychoses. Unfortunately the physiological basis of these disorders is not yet agreed upon, but several findings are relevant. Firstly, it is possible to produce states closely resembling psychoses by the use of the kind of drugs mentioned above; to some extent it is also possible to cure the disorders by means of other drugs; the body chemistry of psychotics is different from that of normal people. This all goes to suggest that metabolic changes affecting the contents of the blood-stream are responsible. Secondly, the verbal utterances of psychotics do not make complete nonsense, and it is possible to analyse their meaning and to carry out psychotherapy in some cases; however it is doubtful how far higher-level processes are important in the case of psychotics, and those who have been cured by physical methods of treatment still have the same religious problems, though they are no longer worried about them. It seems likely that psychotics, like takers of drugs, tend to have religious experiences as a result of their physiological condition, but that the detailed content is determined by learning processes.

(3) Many writers have suggested that religion is connected in some way with the sexual instinct. There are certainly a number of statistical and other findings which require explanation: (a) religious people have a lower frequency of sexual behaviour (pp. 121–3), (b) single people are slightly more

religious than married people, (c) mystics have experiences often of a recognizably sexual character, of which the origin can sometimes be traced (p. 152), (d) it is important for happy marriage that the partners should have the same religious beliefs (pp. 124-6), (e) the age of sudden conversions coincides with puberty (pp. 60-62), (f) Catholics and other conservative religious bodies place restrictions on sexual activity; religious contemplatives always have to be celibate. Some of these finds can be accounted for by the Conflict theory, and some by the Frustration theory. The sexual experiences of mystics can also be explained in physiological terms. Leuba (1925) maintains that the mystical ecstasies of the great mystics were really orgasms aroused in sexually deprived young women with hysterical temperaments, resulting from meditation on the figure of male saints or monks. A number of writers have been struck by the resemblance between the burning ecstasies reported by the mystics, and ordinary sexual experience. The language used in mystical writings often makes use of sexual analogies—the writings of St. John of the Cross are a familiar example. There is no direct evidence of course that the great mystics actually had orgasms, but it is certainly possible that sexual feelings can be given a religious interpretation,* in the same way as the effects of certain drugs can. Perhaps sexual love is often idealized in a quasi-religious way, and at its best approaches religion (Boisen, 1955, p. 60). It is worth noting that celibate religious contemplatives sometimes take part in meditations likely to produce sexual arousal and that any bodily feelings would naturally be interpreted as spiritual experiences.

(4) Acute emotional excitement has been found in connexion with religion in violent conversion and on the battlefield. Evidence was produced to show that religious conversions take place more readily the greater the degree of emotional arousal, though the conversions are correspondingly short-lived (pp. 51-56). Sargant (1957) has argued that such conversions are due to the heightened state of suggestibility of emotionally exhausted people, who can be persuaded to accept any beliefs or

---

*Flournoy (1915) gives a fascinating case-study of a woman who had mystical experiences including visions of a male spiritual friend: he gives a psychological analysis of the production of these hallucinations.

suggestions. In addition to a change of belief, these converts undergo a violent religious experience of the kind which is suggested to them. Soldiers in battle are very often helped by prayer, and become more concerned with religion afterwards; on the other hand they do not report mystical experiences, nor do they become more frequent church-goers (pp. 49–51). It is probably best to explain this in the same way as the religious behaviour of old people—a fantasy response to fear of death; it is not the same kind of phenomenon as the others being discussed in this section.

A number of conclusions can be drawn from this discussion of the physiological hypothesis. Firstly, the theory only applies to religious emotional experiences and to religious visions and voices; it is not relevant to everyday religious behaviour and beliefs. Secondly, there does seem to be a variety of evidence that certain physiological states are involved in these experiences; in particular this is the case with the effects of certain drugs, in certain psychotic conditions, with sexual deprivation and emotional fatigue. Thirdly, these states are not experienced as religious, nor do the hallucinations have a religious content, unless this religious interpretation and content are supplied from a higher level of the central nervous system: this may be through 'dynamic' processes, or through suggestion and learning from the environment.

CONCLUSION

No attempt will be made to present a systematic, rounded account of the mechanisms producing religious behaviour and belief. Some of the theories discussed are strongly supported by the evidence, and conversely much of the empirical material reviewed earlier can be explained in terms of them; however there are several unexplained and unexpected findings, and it seems likely that there are many more complexities to be taken into account. It was thought better at this stage to concentrate on the theories which could be simply expressed and easily verified. Consequently there are several theories, such as those of Jung and Fromm, which have not been included. In fact an attempt was made to write sections on these theories, but it was found impossible to make any testable predictions from them.

Again, some psychoanalysts have given far more 'subtle' and complicated explanations than we have attempted, but they have not provided any convincing evidence that these accounts are correct: it is possible to construct a variety of explanations for the same phenomenon, provided that one is not restricted by the requirements of further data.

However, in order to provide some conclusion to the foregoing discussion we have arranged data and theories under four main 'types'. In constructing these types, the practice of sociologists of religion has been followed in distinguishing churches, denominations and sects (Becker and von Wiese, 1932). Consideration of our statistical data has led to some refinement of these types and the invention of a fourth—'liberal bodies'. This four-fold typology can be justified at the descriptive sociological level, in terms of organization and practices, and this has often been done for the three types of the sociologists. It can also be done at the psychological level, as may be seen from an examination of the results summarized here.

(1) *Conservative religion*. Conservatives accept the whole range of traditional Christian beliefs, including belief in the Devil, Hell and the Virgin Birth. God is conceived of as a powerful, forbidding figure who must be feared. Conservatives have a very high rate of public, but not of private, worship and the type has been described in detail by Adorno and others (1950) in their work on the 'authoritarian personality'. Conservatives tend to belong to what sociologists of religion classify as 'Churches' as opposed to 'denominations' or 'sects'.

It has been shown that religious conservatives tend to be authoritarian and extrapunitive in personality and accordingly are prejudiced towards minority groups, have a high rate of delinquency and they have a low rate of sexual activity. While they belong to all social classes, they are statistically below average, which may be related to their low need for achievement. These are the only churches where there are nearly as many men as women, especially in church attendance, for which there is social pressure. Social learning takes place at an early age from parents and Sunday School, and adolescent conversion is rare. While Roman Catholics fall most clearly into this classification, High Anglicans in Britain and Episcopalians and Lutherans in America are similar; these last two groups are

really intermediate between Conservatism and 'Protestantism'
—as defined in the next section.

It has been shown that the theory that God is a projection of
the super-ego applies particularly to members of these churches
(pp. 154–61). The social learning theory also applies more to
these people than to members of other bodies, since their personality structure is more susceptible to social influence, so that
for example they are more likely to accept their parents' beliefs (pp. 40–42).

(2) *Protestantism.* Protestant is used in its usual sense here. It
has been shown that people falling into this category are less
conservative in belief than those in the last, and that they are
more active in private, less in public, worship. More emphasis
is placed on sin and the need for redemption. The classification
corresponds to that described by Weber (1904–5) in his famous
monograph. Protestants tend to belong to 'denominations' as
defined by sociologists.

In personality, Protestants are intropunitive, as is shown by
their high suicide rate, low delinquency rate and susceptibility to
guilt feelings; they are less authoritarian than Catholics, though
more so than non-religious people. There are 25–55 per cent
more women in these groups. Social learning takes place later
than for Conservatives and adolescent conversion is common,
though this is usually gradual nowadays.

Methodists, Presbyterians and low Anglicans come clearly
into this type. Lutherans and Episcopalians resemble both
Protestants and Conservatives. The Baptists resemble both
Protestants and Sect members, particularly the Negro Baptists;
the Congregationalists in Great Britain can be classified as
Protestants, the American Congregationalists are more like
liberals.

It has been shown that the theory that religion relieves guilt
feelings due to a strong super-ego applies particularly to members of denominations (pp. 154–61). The social learning theory
also applies, though less than to members of churches, and the
learning takes place later.

(3) *Sects.* Sect members are fervent fundamentalists with a
particular interest in the distinctive beliefs or practices of their
group. 'Sects' are a familiar type in the sociology of religion,
and Dynes (1955) has constructed a scale for measuring the

Sect-church dimension. In personality, members of sects are more intropunitive than denomination members, and in addition are unstable with hysterical tendencies. There are between 55 and 100 per cent more women than men. Sects begin by the conversion of adults at meetings, but they soon develop Sunday Schools so that learning then occurs at an earlier age, though people must be converted before they are accepted. Sect members belong largely to the working classes and are relatively uneducated.

The groups which fall most clearly into this category are the Pentecostalists, Seventh Day Adventists, Jehovah's Witnesses, and the various 'Holiness' bodies. Some of the American sects such as the Assembly of God and the Disciples of Christ have recently developed into orthodox denominations.

It has been shown that the theory that religion is a response to socio-economic frustration applies to sect members, as also does the relief of guilt theory—since they can be regarded as an extreme type of denomination. Social learning is less important, though a certain kind of evangelism is influential, and later generations of members may be influenced in childhood.

(4) *Liberalism.* Liberalism, as the name implies, is characterized by a disbelief in much of traditional theology—in the Devil, the Virgin Birth, miracles, even in the divinity of Christ. Religious liberals are not concerned with sin and the need for redemption, nor is their God a watching, forbidding, figure. Instead, there is an optimistic view of life, a belief in the perfectibility of man and in his power to shape his own destiny. Liberals do however believe in God and the after-life, and regard Christ as a great moral teacher. They are more concerned with the ethical than the spiritual side of religion, and take an interest in the 'social gospel'. Liberals correspond to William James' 'once-born' or 'healthy-minded' type and to Fromm's 'humanistic religion' (1951).

From the statistical material reviewed earlier, it seems clear that liberalism has become more widespread in the U.S.A. since 1900, and that it is more common in the churches of the upper and upper middle class. In personality, liberals are humanitarian, impunitive and above average in intelligence; they have a low rate of crime, suicide and prejudice. There are about 25 per cent more women than men on average.

Liberalism is to be found in all the middle class Protestant churches in America—particularly the Congregationalists and Unitarians, while the Jews can also be included here. In Britain the Unitarians, Friends and many members of the Church of England are probably liberals.

What are the psychological mechanisms which produce liberal religion? These people are prosperous and well educated —so that the frustration theory is inappropriate; they are low on authoritarianism—ruling out the projection theory; they are not concerned with sin or redemption and are not intropunitive—so that the relief of guilt theory will not work. In a sense, liberals are simply less religious than the previous types considered, but they do have certain basic beliefs and they do have strong ethical and humanitarian concerns. One possible explanation is that liberal churches primarily reflect the outlook and ideology of the prosperous middle class, expressed in terms of traditional religion, and combined with a good deal of purely secular activity (pp. 34, 133): this would account for a number of the statistical findings.

REFERENCES

A

ADORNO, T. W., *et al.* 1950. *The Authoritarian Personality*. New York: Harper.

ALLINSMITH, W. AND B. 1948. 'Religious affiliation and politico-economic attitude: a study of eight major U.S. religious groups.' *Pub. Op. Quart.* **12**, 377–89.

ALLPORT, G. W. 1954. *The Nature of Prejudice*. Cambridge, Mass.: Addison-Wesley.

ALLPORT, G. W., GILLESPIE, J. M., AND YOUNG, J. 1948. 'The religion of the post-war college student.' *J. Psychol.* **25**, 3–33.

ALLPORT, G. W., AND KRAMER, B. M. 1946. 'Some roots of prejudice.' *J. Psychol.* **22**, 9–39.

ALLPORT, G. W., AND VERNON, P. E. 1931. 'A test for personal values.' *J. Abnorm. Soc. Psychol.* **26**, 231–48.

ARGYLE, M. 1957. *The Scientific Study of Social Behaviour*. London: Methuen.

ARSENIAN, S. 1943. 'Change in evaluative attitudes during four years of college.' *J. Appl. Psychol.* **27**, 338–49.

B

BARBER, B. 1941. 'Acculturation and Messianic movements.' *Amer. Sociol. Rev.* **6**, 663–9.

BARNETT, L. 1948. 'God and the American people.' *Ladies Home Journal.* **65**, 230–40.

BARTLETT, SIR F. C. 1932. *Remembering*. Cambridge University Press.

BECKER, H., AND VON WIESE, L. 1932. *Systematic Sociology*. New York: Wiley.

BELL, H. M. 1938. *Youth Tell Their Story*. New York: Amer. Coun. Educ.

BENDER, L., AND YARRELL, Z. 1938. 'Psychoses among followers of Father Divine.' *J. Nerv. Ment. Dis.* **87**, 418–49.

BERNARD, J. 1949. 'The Rosenzweig picture-frustration study. I. Norms, reliability, and statistical evaluation.' *J. Psychol.* **28**, 325–32.

BETTS, G. 1929. *The Beliefs of 700 Ministers*. New York: Abingdon.

BLUM, G. S. 1949. 'A study of the psychoanalytic theory of psychosexual development.' *Genet. Psychol. Monogr.* **39**, 3–99.

BOISEN, A. T. 1955. *Religion in Crisis and Custom*. New York: Harper.

BONGER, W. A. 1943. *Race and Crime*. Trans. M. M. Hordyk. Columbia U.P.

BOOTH, C. 1902. *Life and Labour of the People in London*. London: Macmillan.

BOSE, R. G. 1929. 'Religious concepts of children.' *Relig. Educ.* **24**, 831–37.

BOVET, P. 1928. *The Child's Religion*. Trans. G. H. Green. London: Dent.

British Institute of Public Opinion (B.I.P.O.)—unpublished reports of surveys 1948, 1950, 1957.

British Weekly. 1955. 'The decline of Nonconformity.' 10th and 17th March.

BROWN, D. G., AND LOWE, W. L. 1951. 'Religious beliefs and personality characteristics of college students.' *J. Soc. Psychol.* **33**, 103–29.

BRUNNER, E. DE S., AND LORGE, I. 1937. *Rural Trends in Depression Years.* Columbia U.P.

BUCKE, R. M. 1901. *Cosmic Consciousness.* New York: Dutton.

BURCHINAL, L. G. 1957. 'Marital satisfaction and religious behaviour.' *Amer. Sociol. Rev.* **22**, 306–10.

BURGESS, E. W., AND COTTRELL, L. S. 1939. *Predicting Success or Failure in Marriage.* New York: Prentice-Hall.

BURTT, H. E., AND FALKENBURG, D. R. JR. 1941. 'The influence of majority and expert opinion on religious attitudes.' *J. Soc. Psychol.* **14**, 269–78.

C

CAMERON, N. 1947. *The Psychology of Behaviour Disorders.* Boston: Houghton Mifflin.

CANTRIL, H. (assisted by H. GAUDET AND H. HERTZOG). 1940. *The Invasion from Mars.* Princeton U.P.

CANTRIL, H. 1941. *The Psychology of Social Movements.* London: Chapman & Hall.

CANTRIL, H. 1951. (Ed.) *Public Opinion 1935–46.* Princeton U.P.

CARLSON, H. B. 1934. 'Attitudes of undergraduate students.' *J. Soc. Psychol.* **5**, 202–12.

CATTELL, R. B. 1946. *Description and Measurement of Personality.* New York: World Book Co.

CAUTER, T., AND DOWNHAM, J. S. 1954. *The Communication of Ideas.* London: Readers' Digest and Chatto and Windus.

CAVAN, R. S. 1928. *Suicide.* U. of Chicago Press.

CAVAN, R. S. *et al.* 1949. *Personal Adjustment in Old Age.* Chicago: Science Research Associates.

CAVANAUGH, J. J. 1939. 'Survey of fifteen surveys.' *Bull. Univ. Notre Dame.* **34**, 1–128.

Census (1906, 1916, 1926, 1936). *Census of Religious Bodies.* U.S. Dept. of Commerce, Bureau of the Census.

Census. 1940. *16th Census of the United States.* U.S. Dept. of Commerce, Bureau of the Census.

CENTERS, R. 1949. *The Psychology of Social Classes.* Princeton U.P.

CHESSER, E. 1956. *The Sexual, Marital and Family Relationships of the English Woman.* London: Hutchinson.

CHILD, I. L. 1954. 'Socialization.' Chap. 18 in Lindzey. 1954.

CHRISTIE, R., AND JAHODA, M. 1954. *Studies in the Scope and Method of the Authoritarian Personality.* Glencoe, Ill.: The Free Press.

CLARK, E. T. 1929. *The Psychology of Religious Awakening.* New York: Macmillan.

CLARK, E. T. 1949. *The Small Sects in America.* Nashville, N.Y.: Abingdon-Cokesbury.

COCKRUM, L. V. 1952. 'Personality traits and interests of theological students.' *Relig. Educ.* **47**, 28–32.

COE, G. A. 1916. *The Psychology of Religion.* U. of Chicago Press.

COFFIN, T. E. 1944. 'A three-component theory of leadership.' *J. Abnorm. Soc. Psychol.* **39**, 63–83.

COHN, N. 1957. *The Pursuit of the Millenium.* London: Secker and Warburg.

COLQUHOUN, F. 1955. *Harringay Story.* London: Hodder and Stoughton.

COOKE, A. 1955. 'Billy Graham in New York: the prodigal's return.' *Manchester Guardian.* March 7th.

CRAWFORD, B. F. 1938. *Religious Trends in a Century of Hymns.* New York: Carnegie Press.

CRONIN, H. J. 1934. 'Psychoanalytic sources of religious conflicts.' *Med. Rec.* **139**, 32–34.

CRUTCHFIELD, R. S. 1955. 'Conformity and character.' *Amer. Psychol.* **10**, 191–8.

D

DAVENPORT, F. M. 1906. *Primitive Traits in Religious Revivals.* New York: Macmillan.

DAYTON, N. A. 1940. *New Facts on Mental Disorders.* Springfield, Ill.: Charles C. Thomas.

DOUGLASS, H. P. 1926. *1000 City Churches.* New York: Doran.

DREGER, R. M. 1952. 'Some personality correlates of religious attitudes as determined by projective techniques.' *Psychol. Monogr.* **66**, No. 3.

DUBLIN, L. I. 1933. *To be or not to be.* New York: Smith and Haas.

DUDYCHA, G. J. 1950. 'The religious beliefs of college freshmen in 1930 and 1949.' *Relig. Educ.* **45**, 165–9.

DURKHEIM, E. 1897. *Suicide.* Trans. J. A. Spaulding and G. Simpson. London: Routledge and Kegan Paul.

DYNES, R. R. 1955. 'Church-sect typology and socio-economic status.' *Amer. Sociol. Rev.* **20**, 555–60.

E

ELLIOTT, M. A. 1952. *Crime in Modern Society.* New York: Harper.

ELLIS, A. 1946. 'The validity of personality questionnaires.' *Psychol. Bull.* **43**, 385–440.

EYSENCK, H. J. 1944. 'General social attitudes.' *J. Soc. Psychol.* **19**, 207–27.

EYSENCK, H. J. 1947. *Dimensions of Personality.* London: Kegan Paul.

EYSENCK, H. J. 1953. *The Structure of Human Personality.* London: Methuen.

EYSENCK, H. J. 1954. *Psychology of Politics.* London: Routledge.

F

FARR, C. B., AND HOWE, R. L. 1932. 'The influence of religious ideas on the etiology, symptomology, and prognosis of the psychoses. With special reference to social factors.' *Amer. J. Psychiat.* **11**, 845–65.

FARRELL, B. A. 1955. 'Psychological theory and the belief in God.' *Int. J. Psycho-Anal.* **36**, 1–18.

FENICHEL, O. 1945. *The Psychoanalytic Theory of Neurosis.* New York: Norton.

FERGUSON, L. W. 1944. 'Socio-psychological correlates of the primary attitude scales. I. Religionism. II. Humanitarianism.' *J. Soc. Psychol.* **19**, 81–98.

FERGUSON, T. 1952. *The Young Delinquent in his Social Setting.* Oxford U.P.

FESTINGER, L. (1954). 'A theory of social comparison processes.' *Hum. Rel.* **7**, 117–40.

FESTINGER, L. *et al.* 1956. *When Prophecy Fails.* U. of Minnesota Press.

FICHTER, J. H. 1952. 'The profile of Catholic religious life.' *Amer. J. Sociol.* **58**, 145–9.

FISHER, SIR R. A., AND YATES, F. 1938. *Statistical Tables for Biological, Agricultural and Medical Research.* Edinburgh: Oliver and Boyd.

FISHER, S. C. 1948. 'Relationships in attitudes, opinions and values among family members.' *Univ. Calif. Pub. Cult. Soc.* **2**, 29–100.

FLECK, U. 1935. 'Uber Relgiostät der Epileptiker.' *Arch. Psychiat. Nervenkr.* **103**, 122–35.

FLOURNOY, T. 1915. 'Une mystique moderne.' *Arch. de Psychol.* **15**, 42–45.

FLOWER, J. C. 1927. *An Approach to the Psychology of Religion.* London; Kegan Paul.

FLUGEL, J. C. 1945. *Man, Morals and Society.* London: Duckworth.

FRANZBLAU, A. N. 1934. *Religious Belief and Character among Jewish Adolescents.* Teach. Coll. Contr. Educ. no. 634.

FREEDMAN, R., AND WHELPTON, P. K. 1950. 'Social and psychological factors affecting fertility. X. Fertility planning and fertility rates of religious interest and denomination.' *Millbank Mem. Fd. Quart.* **28**, 294–343.

FRENCH, V. V. 1947. 'The structure of sentiments. III. A study of philosophico-religious sentiments.' *J. Pers.* **16**, 209–44.

FREUD, S. 1907. 'Obsessive acts and religious practices.' *Coll. Papers* **2**, 25–35.

FREUD, S. 1927. *The Future of an Illusion.* London: Hogarth Press.

FREUD, S. 1933. *New Introductory Lectures on Psychoanalysis.* London: Hogarth Press.

FREUD, S. 1939. *Civilisation and its Discontents.* London: Hogarth Press.

FRITSCH, F., AND HETZER, H. 1928. 'Die religiose Entwicklung des Jugendlichen.' *Arch. f. d. ges. Psychol.* **62**, 409–42.

FROMM, E. 1951. *Psychoanalysis and Religion.* London: Gollancz.

FRY, C. L. 1933. 'The religious affiliations of American leaders.' *Scient. Mo.* **36**, 241–9.

FRY, L. F., AND JESSUP, M. F. 1933. 'Changes in religious organisations.' Chap. 20, in *Recent Social Trends in the United States.* New York: McGraw-Hill.

FUNK, R. A. 1956. 'Religious attitudes and manifest anxiety in a college population.' (Abstract) *Amer. Psychol.* **11**, 375.

G

GADOUREK, I. 1956. *A Dutch Community.* Leiden: Stenfert Kroese.

GARRISON, K. C. 1951. *Psychology of Adolescence.* New York: Prentice-Hall.

GILLILAND, A. R. 1940. 'The attitude of college students toward God and the church.' *J. Soc. Psychol.* **11**, 11–18.

GILLILAND, A. R. 1953. 'Changes in religious beliefs of college students.' *J. Soc. Psychol.* **37**, 113–6.

GILLIN, J. L. 1945. *Criminology and Penology.* New York: Appleton-Century.

GLUECK, S. AND E. 1950. *Unravelling Juvenile Delinquency*. London: Oxford U.P.

GOLDSCHMIDT, W. R. 1944. 'Class denominations in rural California churches.' *Amer. J. Sociol.* **49**, 348–55.

GORER, G. 1955. *Exploring English Character*. London: Cresset.

GREGORY. 1957. 'Are we still Christians?' *News Chronicle*. 15th–17th April.

GRUBB, K. G., AND BINGLE, E. J. 1949. *World Christian Handbook*. London: World Dominion Press.

GUILFORD, J. P. 1950. *Fundamental statistics in Psychology and Education*. New York: McGraw-Hill.

H

HALBWACHS, M. 1930. *Les Causes du Suicide*. Paris: Librairie Félix Alcan.

HALL, G. S. 1905. *Adolescence*. London: Sidney Appleton.

HARDING, J. *et al.* 1954. 'Prejudice and ethnic relations.' Chap. 27 in Lindzey (1954).

HARE, E. H. 1952. 'The ecology of mental disease.' *J. Ment. Sci.* **98**, 579–94.

HARMS, E. 1944. 'The development of religious experience in children.' *Amer. J. Sociol.* **50**, 112–22.

HART, H. 1933. 'Changing social attitudes and interests.' Chap. 8 in *Recent Social Trends in the United States*. New York: McGraw-Hill.

HART, H. 1942. 'Religion.' *Amer. J. Sociol.* **47**, 888–97.

HARTMANN, G. W. 1936. 'A field experiment on the comparative effectiveness of "emotional" and "rational" political leaflets in determining election results.' *J. Abnorm. Soc. Psychol.* **13**, 54–57.

HEALY, W., AND BRONNER, A. F. 1936. *New Light on Delinquency and its Treatment*.

HENDERSON, D., AND GILLESPIE, R. D. 1956. *A Textbook of Psychiatry*. Oxford U.P.

HENRY, A. F., AND SHORT, J. F. 1954. *Homicide and Suicide*. Glencoe, Ill.: The Free Press.

HERBERG, W. 1955. *Protestant-Catholic-Jew*. New York: Doubleday.

HERRON, S. 1955. 'What's left of Harringay?' *British Weekly*, Feb. 10th.

HIGHET, J. 1957. 'The churches in Glasgow.' *British Weekly*, August 22nd, 29th.

HIGHTOWER, P. R. 1930. 'Biblical information in relation to character and conduct.' *Univ. Ia. Stud. Char.* **3**, No. 2.

HIRSCHBERG, G., AND GILLILAND, A. R. 1942. 'Parent-child relations in attitudes.' *J. Abnorm. Soc. Psychol.* **37**, 125–30.

HOFFMAN, M. L. 1953. 'Some psychodynamic factors in compulsive conformity.' *J. Abnorm. Soc. Psychol.* **48**, 383–93.

HOLLINGWORTH, L. S. 1933. 'The adolescent child.' pp. 882–908 in Murchison, *A Handbook of Child Psychology*. Clark U.P.

HOLT, J. B. 1940. 'Holiness religion: cultural shock and social reorganisation.' *Amer. Sociol. Rev.* **5**, 740–7.

HORNEY, K. 1946. *Our Inner Conflicts*. London: Lund Humphries.

HORTON, P. B. 1940. 'Student interest in the church.' *Relig. Educ.* **35**, 215–9.

HOVLAND, C. I. 1954. 'Effects of the mass media of communication.' Chap. 28 in Lindzey (1954).

HOWELLS. T. H. 1928. 'A comparative study of those who accept as against those who reject religious authority.' *Univ. Ia. Stud. Char.* **2**, No. 2.

HUNT, J. MCV. 1938. 'An instance of the social origin of conflict resulting in psychoses.' *Amer. J. Orthopsychiat.* **8**, 158–64.

HUXLEY, A. 1954. *Doors of Perception*. London: Chatto and Windus.

HYDE, K. E. *et al.* 1956. *Sunday Schools Today*. London: Free Church Federal Council.

I

ILSAGER, H. 1949. 'Factors influencing the formation and change of political and religious attitudes.' *J. Soc. Psychol.* **29**, 253–65.

INFORMATION SERVICE. 1948. 'Christianity and the Economic order.' No. 10. Social-economic status and the outlook of religious groups in America.' May 15th.

INFORMATION SERVICE. 1954. 'Trends in giving to 14 religious bodies.' Oct. 2nd. National Council of the churches of Christ in the U.S.A.

J

JAMES, W. 1902. *The Varieties of Religious Experience*. New York: Longmans.

JANIS, I. L. 1954. 'Personality correlates of susceptibility to persuasion. *J. Pers.* **22**, 504–18.

JEFFREYS, J. B., AND WALTERS, D. 1956. 'National income and expenditure of the United Kingdom 1870–1952.' *Nat. Inst. of Econ. and Soc. Res. Reprint Series*. No. 6.

JOAD, C. E. M. 1930. *The Present and Future of Religion*. London: Benn.

JOHNSON, E. H. 1943. 'Personality traits of workers in the field of religion.' *Relig. Educ.* **38**, 325–9.

JONES, V. 1936. 'Attitudes of college students towards war, race and religion and the changes in such attitudes during four years in college.' *Psychol. Bull.* **33**, 731–2.

JONES, W. L. 1937. *A Psychological Study of Religious Conversion*. London: Epworth Press.

JUNG, C. G. 1933. *Modern Man in Search of a Soul*. London: Kegan Paul.

K

KARDINER, A. *et al.* 1945. *The Psychological Frontiers of Society*. New York: Columbia U.P.

KARLSSON, G. 1957. *Adaptability and Communication in Marriage*. Uppsala: Almquist & Wiksells Boktrycheri ab.

KATZ, D., AND ALLPORT, F. H. 1931. *Students' Attitudes*. Syracuse, N.Y.: Craftsman Press.

KAUFMAN, M. R. 1939. 'Religious delusions in schizophrenia.' *Int. J. Psycho-Anal.* **20**, 363–76.

KELLY, E. L., AND FISKE, D. W. 1951. *The Selection of Clinical Psychologists.* U. of Michigan Press.

KIMBER, J. A. M. 1947. 'Interests and personality of Bible Institute students.' *J. Soc. Psychol.* **26**, 225–33.

KINCHELOE, S. C. 1937. *Research Memorandum on Religion in the Depression. S.S.R.C. Bull.* No. 33.

KING, S. H., AND FUNKENSTEIN, D. H. 1957. 'Religious practice and cardio-vascular reactions during stress.' *J. Abnorm. Soc. Psychol.* **55**, 135–7.

KINGSBURY, F.A. 1937. 'Why do people go to church?' *Relig. Educ.* **32**, 50–54.

KINSEY, A. C. *et al.* 1948. *Sexual Behaviour in the Human Male.* London: Saunders.

KINSEY, A. C. 1953. *Sexual Behaviour in the Human Female.* London: Saunders.

KIRKPATRICK, C. 1949. 'Religion and humanitarianism: a study of institutional implications.' *Psychol. Monogr.* **63**, No. 9.

KITAY, P.M. 1947. *Radicalism and Conservatism toward conventional religion: a Psychological Study based on a group of Jewish College Students.* Teach. Coll. Contr. Educ. No. 919.

KLÜVER, H. 1928. *Mescal.* London: Kegan Paul.

KNAPP, R. H., AND GOODRICH, H. B. 1951. 'The origins of American scientists.' *Science.* **113**, 543–5.

KUHLEN, R. G., AND ARNOLD, M. 1944. 'Age differences in religious beliefs and problems during adolescence.' *J. Genet. Psychol.* **65**, 291–300.

KUPKY, O. 1928. *The Religious Development of Adolescents.* New York: Macmillan.

L

LA BARRE, W. 1938. *The Peyote Cult.* New York: Yale U.P.

LANDIS, J. T. 1949. 'Marriages of mixed and non-mixed religious faith.' *Amer. Sociol. Rev.* **14**, 401–7.

LANDIS, J. T. AND M. G. 1953. *Building a Successful Marriage.* New York: Prentice-Hall.

LAZARSFELD, P. F. *et al.* 1944. *The People's Choice.* New York: Duell, Sloan and Pearce.

LAZARSFELD, P. F. 1955. 'Interpretation of statistical relations as a research operation.' 115–25 in P. F. Lazarsfeld and M. Rosenberg *The Language of Social Research.* Glencoe, Ill.: The Free Press.

LENSKI, G. E. 1953. 'Social correlates of religious interest.' *Amer. Sociol. Rev.* **18**, 533–44.

LEUBA, J. H. 1921. *The Belief in God and Immortality.* Chicago: Open Court Pub. Co.

LEUBA, J. H. 1925. *The Psychology of Religious Mysticism.* London: Kegan Paul.

LEUBA, J. H. 1934. 'Religious beliefs of American scientists.' *Harper's* **169**, 297.

LINDZEY, G. (ed.) 1954. *Handbook of Social Psychology.* Cambridge, Mass.: Addison-Wesley.

LIPSET, S. M. 1953. 'Opinion formation in a crisis situation.' *Pub. Op. Quart.* **17**, 20–46.

LIPSET, S. M. *et al* 1954. 'The psychology of voting: an analysis of political behaviour.' Chap. 30 in Lindzey (1954).

LOCKE, H. J. 1951. *Predicting Adjustment in Marriage*. New York: Holt.

LOMBROSO, C. 1911. *Crime. Its cause and Remedies*. Trans. H. P. Horton. London: Heinemann.

LUBELL, S. 1956. *Revolt of the Moderates*. New York: Harper.

M

MCCARTHY, T. J. 1942. 'Personality traits of seminarians.' *Stud. Psychol. Cath. Univ. Amer.* **5**, No. 4.

MCKEEFERY, W. J. 1949. 'A critical analysis of quantitative studies of religious awakening.' Unpublished Ph.D. thesis, Union Theol. Seminary and Teach. Coll.

MCKELLAR, P. 1957. *Imagination and Thinking*. London: Cohen and West.

MACLAY, W. S., AND GUTTMAN, E. 1941. 'Mescaline hallucinations in artists.' *Arch. Neur. Psychiat.* **45**, 130–7.

MCCLELLAND, D. C. 1955. 'Some social consequences of achievement motivation.' *Nebraska Symposium on Motivation*. U. of Nebraska Press.

MCCOMB, S. 1928. 'Spiritual healing in Europe.' *Ment. Hygiene* **12**, 706–21.

MADGE, J. 1953. *The Tools of Social Science*. London: Longmans.

MALINOWSKI, B. 1925. *Science, Religion and Reality*. Ed. by J. Needham. New York: Macmillan.

Mass Observation. 1947. *Puzzled People*. London: Gollancz.

MATTHEWS, R. 1936. *English Messiahs*. London: Methuen.

MAYER-GROSS, W. 1951. 'Experimental psychoses and other abnormalities produced by drugs.' *Brit. Med. J.* **2**, 317–20.

MAYER-GROSS, W., SLATER, E., AND ROTH, M. 1954. *Clinical Psychiatry*. London: Cassell.

MIDDLETON, W. C., AND FAY, P. J. 1941. 'Attitudes of delinquent and non-delinquent girls toward Sunday observance, the Bible, and war.' *J. Educ. Psychol.* **32**, 555–8.

MINER, J. R. 1931. 'Church membership and commitments of prisoners.' *Hum. Biol.* **3**, 429–36.

MITCHELL, S. W. 1896. 'Remarks on the effects of Anhelonium Lewinii.' *Brit. Med. J.* **2**, 1625–9.

MOBERG, D. O. 1953. 'The Christian religion and personal adjustment in old age.' *Amer. Sociol. Rev.* **18**, 87–90.

MONAHAN, T. P., AND KEPHART, W. M. 1954. 'Divorce and desertion by religious and mixed-religious groups.' *Amer. J. Sociol.* **59**, 454–65.

MORETON, F. E. 1944. 'Attitudes to religion among adolescents and adults.' *Brit. J. Educ. Psychol.* **14**, 69–79.

MOWRER, E. R. 1927. *Family Disorganisation*. U. of Chicago Press.

MUDIE-SMITH, R. 1904. *The Religious Life of London*. London: Hodder and Stoughton.

MURPHY, G. MURPHY, L. B., AND NEWCOMB, T. M. 1937. *Experimental Social Psychology*. New York: Harper.

MURRAY, H. A. 1938. *Explorations in Personality*. New York: Oxford U.P.

MYRDAL, G. 1944. *An American Dilemma*. New York: Harper.

N

NATHAN, M. 1932. *The Attitude of the Jewish Student in the Colleges and Universities towards his Religion*. New York: Bloch.

NEWCOMB, T. M. 1943. *Personality and Social Change*. New York: Dryden.

NEWCOMB, T. M., AND SVEHLA, G. 1937. 'Intra-family relationships in attitude.' *Sociometry*. **1**, 180–205.

NIEBUHR, H. R. 1929. *The Social Sources of Denominationalism*. New York: Holt.

NOTTINGHAM, E. K. 1954. *Religion and Society*. New York: Doubleday.

NOWLAN, E. H. 1957. 'The picture of the "Catholic" which emerges from attitude tests.' *Lumen Vitae*. **12**, 275–85.

O

OATES, W. 1949. 'The role of religion in the psychoses,' *J. Pastoral Care*. **3**. 21–30.

OATES, W. 1957. *Religious Factors in Mental Illness*. London: Allen and Unwin.

Odham. 1947. Unpublished report on survey. Odham's Press.

OGBURN, W. F., AND TIBBITS, C. 1933. 'The Family and its Functions.' Chap. 13 in *Recent Social Trends*. New York: McGraw-Hill.

OLT, R. 1956. *An Approach to the Psychology of Religion*. Boston: Christopher.

OSMOND, H., AND SMITHIES, J. 1952. 'Schizophrenia: a new approach.' *J. Ment. Sci.* **98**, 309–15.

P

PARRY, H. J. 1949. 'Protestants, Catholics and prejudice.' *Int. J. Op. Att. Res.* **3**, 205–13.

PEARCE, J. D. W. 1952. *Juvenile Delinquency*. London: Cassell.

PEARL, R. 1931. 'Some notes on the census of religious bodies, 1926.' *J. Soc. Psychol.* **2**, 417–32.

PEARSON, G. B., AND FERGUSON, J. O. 1953. 'Nun's melancholy.' 382–9 in *Encyclopedia of Aberrations*. Ed. E. Podolsky. New York: Philosophical Library.

PENROSE, L. S. 1952. *On the Objective Study of Crowd Behaviour*. London: H. K. Lewis.

PETERS, R. 1942. 'A study of the intercorrelations of personality traits among a group of novices in religious communities.' *Stud. Psychol. Psychiat. Cath. Univ. Amer.* **5**, No. 7.

PFAUTZ, H. W. 1955. 'The sociology of secularization: religious groups.' *Amer. J. Sociol.* **61**, 121–8.

PFISTER, O. 1948. *Christianity and Fear*. New York: Macmillan.

PHILP, H. L. 1956. *Freud and Religious Belief*. London: Rockliff.

PIDDINGTON, R. 1950. *An Introduction to Social Anthropology*. Edinburgh: Oliver and Boyd.

POPE, L. 1942. *Millhands and Preachers*. Yale U.P.

POPE, L. 1948. 'Religion and the class structure.' *Ann. Amer. Acad. Pol. Soc. Sci.* **256**, 84–91.

PRATT, J. B. 1924. *The Religious Consciousness*. New York: Macmillan.

PRATT, K. C. 1937. 'Differential selection of intelligence according to denominational preference of college freshmen.' *J. Soc. Psychol.* **8**, 301–10.

PRESSEY, S. L., AND KUHLEN, R. G. 1957. *Psychological Development through the Life Span*. New York: Harper.

PROTHRO, E. T., AND JENSEN, J. A. 1950. 'Interrelations of religious and ethnic attitudes in selected southern populations.' *J. Soc. Psychol.* **32**, 45–49.

R

REIK, T. 1951. *Dogma and Compulsion*. New York: International Univ. Press.

RINGER, B. J., AND GLOCK, C. Y. 1955. 'The political role of the church as defined by its parishioners.' *Pub. Op. Quart.* **18**, 337–47.

ROBERTS, B. H., AND MYERS, J. K. 1954. 'Religion, national origin, immigration and mental illness.' *Amer. J. Psychiat.* **110**, 759–64.

ROMMETVEIT, R. 1955. *Social Norms and Roles*. Oslo: Akademeik Forlag.

ROSANDER, A. C. 1939. 'Age and sex patterns of social attitudes.' *J. Educ. Psychol.* **30**, 481–96.

ROSE, A. M. 1956. *Mental Health and Mental Disorder*. London: Routledge and Kegan Paul.

ROSENZWEIG, S. 1945 .'The picture-association method and its application in a study of reaction to frustration.' *J. Pers.* **14**, 3–23.

ROSS, M. G. 1950. *Religious Beliefs of Youth*. New York: Association Press.

ROSTEN, L. 1955. *A Guide to the Religions of America*. New York: Simon and Schuster.

ROWNTREE, B. S., AND LAVERS, G. R. 1957. *English Life and Leisure*. London: Longmans.

S

SANAI, M. 1952. 'An empirical study of political, religious and social attitudes.' *Brit. J. Psychol.* (statist. section). **5**, 81–92.

SANFORD, F. H. 1950. *Authoritarianism and Leadership*. Philadelphia: Inst. for Research in Hum. Relat.

SAPPENFIELD, B. R. 1942. 'The attitudes of Catholic, Protestant and Jewish students.' *J. Soc. Psychol.* **16**, 173–97.

SARGENT, W. 1957. *Battle for the Mind*. London: Heinemann.

SCHANK, R. L. 1932. 'A study of a community and its groups and institutions conceived of as behaviour of individuals.' *Psychol. Monogr.* **43**, no. 195.

SEARS, R. R. 1943. *Survey of Objective Studies of Psychoanalytic Concepts*. S.S.R.C. Bull. No. 51.

SHUTTLEWORTH, F. K. 1927. 'The influence of early religious home training on college sophomore men.' *Relig. Educ.* **2**, 57–60.

SINCLAIR, R. D. 1928. 'A comparative study of those who report the experience of the divine presence and those who do not.' *Univ. Ia. Stud. Char.* **2**, No. 3.

SLATER, E. 1947. 'Neurosis and religious affiliation.' *J. Ment. Sci.* **93**, 392–8.

SMITH, K. 1953. 'Distribution-free statistical methods and the concept of power efficiency.' Chap. 12 in Festinger, L., and Katz, D. *Research Methods in the Behavioral Sciences.* New York: Dryden.

SMITH, M. B., BRUNER, J. S., AND WHITE, R. W. 1956. *Opinions and Personality.* New York: Wiley.

SMITH, R. O. 1947. *Factors affecting the Religion of College Students.* Ann. Arbor, Mich.: Lane Hall.

SNEDECOR, G. W. 1937. *Statistical Methods.* Iowa State Univ. Press.

SPOERL, D. T. 1951. 'Some aspects of prejudice as affected by religion and education.' *J. Soc. Psychol.* **33**, 69–76.

SPOERL, D. T. 1952. 'The values of the post war college student.' *J. Soc. Psychol.* **35**, 217–25.

STARBUCK, E. D. 1899. *The Psychology of Religion.* London: Walter Scott.

STARBUCK, E. D. 1926. 'An empirical study of mysticism.' *Proc. 6th Int. Cong. Phil.* 87–94.

STOCKINGS, G. T. 1940. 'A clinical study of the mescaline psychosis.' *J. Ment. Sci.* **86**, 29–47.

STOCKWOOD, M. 1953. 'The Redfield United Front survey.' *Redfield Review*, May and June.

STONE, S. 1934. 'The Miller delusion: a comparative study in mass psychology.' *Amer. J. Psychiat.* **91**, 593–623.

STOUFFER, S. A. *et al.* 1949. *The American Soldier. Vol. II. Combat and its Aftermath.* Princeton U.P.

SUPER, D. E. 1957. *The Psychology of Careers.* New York: Harper.

SUTHERLAND, E. H. 1939. *Principles of Criminology.* Chicago: Lippincott.

SWARD, K. 1931. 'Temperament and religious experience.' *J. Soc. Psychol.* **2**, 374–96.

SWEET, W. W. 1948. 'The Protestant Churches.' *Ann. Amer. Acad Pol. Soc. Sci.* **256**, 43–52.

SYMINGTON, T. A. 1935. *Religious Liberals and Conservatives.* Teach. Coll. Contr. Educ. No. 640.

T

TELFORD, C. W. 1950. 'A study of religious attitudes.' *J. Soc. Psychol.* **31**, 217–30.

TERMAN, L. M. 1938. *Psychological Factors in Marital Happiness.* New York: McGraw-Hill.

TERMAN, L. M., AND MILES, C. C. 1936. *Sex and Personality.* New York: McGraw-Hill.

THOULESS, R. H. 1924. *An Introduction to the Psychology of Religion.* Cambridge U.P.

THOULESS, R. H. 1935. 'The tendency to certainty in religious belief.' *Brit. J. Psychol.* **26**, 16–31.

THURSTON, H. 1951. *The Physical Phenomena of Mysticism.* London: Burns Oates.

THURSTONE, L. L., AND CHAVE, E. J. 1929. *The Measurement of Attitude.* U. of Chicago Press.

TITUS, H. E., AND HOLLANDER, E. P. 1957. 'The California F Scale in psychological research. 1950–1955.' *Psychol. Bull.* **54**, 47–64.

TOYNBEE, SIR A. 1946. *A Study of History.* Abridged version of vols. 1–6 by D. C. Somervell. London: Oxford U.P.

TRENAMAN, J. 1952. *Out of Step.* London: Methuen.

U

UNDERHILL, E. 1911. *Mysticism.* London: Methuen.

UNWIN, J. D. 1934. *Sex and Culture.* Oxford U.P.

W

WARNER, W. L., AND LUNT, P. S. 1941. *The Social Life of a Modern Community.* New Haven: Yale U.P.

WEATHERHEAD, L. D. 1951. *Psychology, Religion and Healing.* London: Hodder and Stoughton.

WEBER, M. 1904–5. *The Protestant Ethic and the Spirit of Capitalism.* Trans. T. Parsons, London: Allen and Unwin. 1930.

WELFORD, A. T. 1947. 'Is religious behavior dependent upon affect or frustration?' *J. Abnorm. Soc. Psychol.* **42**, 310–19.

WEYGANDT, W. 1926. 'Zur Psychopathologie der Sektenbildung.' Bekhterev 40th anniv. commem. volume.

WICKHAM, E. R. 1957. *Church and People in an Industrial City.* London: Lutterworth.

WILKE, W. H. 1934. 'An experimental comparison of the speech, the radio and the printed page as propaganda devices.' *Arch. Psychol.* No. 169.

WILSON, B. R. 1955. 'Social aspects of religious sects: a study of some contemporary sects in Great Britain.' Unpub. Ph.D. thesis London Univ.

WINTERBOTTOM, M. 1953. 'The sources of achievement motivation in mothers' attitudes towards independence training.' pp. 297–304 in McClelland *et al. The Achievement Motive.* N.Y.: Appleton-Century-Crofts.

WOODWARD, L. E. 1932. *Relations of Religious Training and Life Patterns to the Adult Religious Life.* Teach. Coll. Contr. Educ. No. 527.

WOOLSTON, H. 1937. 'Religious consistency.' *Amer. Sociol. Rev.* **2**, 380–8.

Y

Yearbook. 1900–57. *Yearbook of American Churches.* Nat. Coun. of the churches of Christ in the U.S.A. Later vols. edited by B. Y. Landis.

YINGER, J. M. 1957. *Religion, Society and the Individual.* New York: Macmillan.

Z

ZAEHNER, R. C. 1957. *Mysticism, Sacred and Profane.* Oxford U.P.

ZIMMERMAN, F. K. 1934. 'Religion and conservative social force.' *J. Abnorm. Soc. Psychol.* **28**, 473–4.

ZUBIN, J. 1939. 'Nomographs for determining the significance of the differences between the frequencies of events in two contrasted series or groups.' *J. Amer. Stat. Ass.* **34**, 539–44.

INDEX OF NAMES

SUBJECT INDEX

194